Praise for Bess Kalb

NOBODY WILL TELL YOU THIS BUT ME

"I have never read anything that feels truer to my experience of having a Jewish grandmother than *Nobody Will Tell You This But Me*." —Emily Burack, *Hey Alma*

"Lively and fascinating, funny yet poignant. . . . Kalb . . . pulls off [a] daring approach brilliantly. . . . In a bold stroke of literary bravura, [she] has turned the formula for writing memoirs inside out, bringing her grandmother's distinctive voice back to life and sharing it with a legion of lucky readers. . . . Enthralling." —*BookPage* (starred review)

"An endearing, bittersweet, and entertainingly fresh take on the family memoir. . . . The narrative skillfully captures Bobby's wit, worldly advice, well-intentioned meddling, and enduring love for her granddaughter." —*Kirkus Reviews* (starred review)

"Charming, hilarious, and ever-quotable. . . . An uncanny rendering of two whole, wholly connected women and their unshakable bond." —*Booklist* (starred review)

"Kalb deftly captures her grandmother's fierce, loving, and particular personality. . . . Striking a perfect balance between levity and poignancy, this is a standout debut." —*Library Journal* (starred review)

"A love story that resonates across generations. . . . Original, moving and funny." —*The Florida Times-Union*

Bess Kalb

NOBODY WILL TELL YOU THIS BUT ME

Bess Kalb is an Emmy-nominated writer for *Jimmy Kimmel Live!* Her writing for the show earned her a Writer's Guild Award in 2016. She has also written for the Oscars and the Emmys. A regular contributor to *The New Yorker*'s Daily Shouts, her work has been published in *The New Republic, Grantland, Salon, Wired, The Nation,* and elsewhere. She lives in Los Angeles.

www.besskalb.com

NOBODY
WILL TELL YOU
THIS
BUT ME

NOBODY WILL TELL YOU THIS BUT ME

· a true (as told to me) story ·

BESS KALB

VINTAGE BOOKS

A DIVISION OF PENGUIN RANDOM HOUSE LLC

NEW YORK

FIRST VINTAGE BOOKS EDITION, APRIL 2021

The Library of Congress has cataloged the Knopf edition as follows:
Names: Kalb, Bess, 1987– author.
Title: Nobody will tell you this but me : a true (as told to me) story / Bess Kalb.
Description: First edition. | New York : Alfred A. Knopf, 2020.
Identifiers: LCCN 2019026101 (print) | LCCN 2019026102 (ebook)
Subjects: LCSH: Kalb, Bess, 1987– | Grandmothers—Anecdotes. Grandparent and
child—Anecdotes.
Classification: LCC HQ759.9 .K36 2020 (print) | LCC HQ759.9 (ebook) | DDC
306.874/5—dc23
LC record available at https://lccn.loc.gov/2019026101
LC ebook record available at https://lccn.loc.gov/2019026102

Vintage Books Trade Paperback ISBN: 978-0-525-56382-2
eBook ISBN: 978-0-525-65472-8

Author photograph © Lucas Foglia
Book design by Maggie Hinders

www.vintagebooks.com

Printed in the United States of America
10 9 8 7 6 5 4 3 2 1

Thank you, Grandma.
And for my son.

CONTENTS

PROLOGUE

I COULD TELL THIS GIRL she'd marry the love of her life in a year. She'd leave the tenement in Brooklyn and see Cairo and Tuscany and China and Switzerland and Greece and Gaza and Paris—Paris more times than she could count. She'd visit her mother's village in Belarus (then part of Russia), the village her mother fled when she was thirteen years old, and that night she'd order a Kir Royale at the hotel bar. She'd have two worshipful sons and one daughter.

. . .

Her daughter would be her spitting image, as if she were reborn. She'd teach her daughter to study harder than her sons. To speak louder. To make 'em laugh to make 'em relax. She'd read her daughter Emily Brontë at night. Her daughter would be in the first class of women admitted to Brown. Her daughter would graduate by twenty. Her daughter would say, "I want to be a doctor," and she'd tell her, "Go be a doctor." Her daughter had never taken science.

.   .   .

Her daughter became a doctor. Her daughter would have a daughter, me.

.   .   .

She and I would fall in love. We'd speak in songs: *"My angel, my angel, you saved my life."* We'd have secrets and hiding places and code words. We'd talk about our hair until we fell asleep. We'd watch old movies and read new books. We'd cry for no reason. We'd cry for every reason all at once. We'd said everything that ever occurred to us to each other, even if it was nothing, or mean, or so mean it was crazy. We'd eat the same foods at exactly the same rates in exactly the same ways. We never said goodbye, always "I love you, I love you, I love you." Three times. Never enough. "If you ever have a daughter," she'd tell me, "I declare her a force."

MY FUNERAL

It's a terrible thing to be dead. Oh, how boring. How maddening. Nothing to do. Nothing to read. No one to talk to. And everyone's a mess. Thank God for that, at least. The rabbi at the service didn't know me from Adam. I didn't pay attention.

I was watching your grandfather. I always hated Hebrew—Bessie, there was too much of it!—but when everyone started the chants he finally stopped crying. Fine. Good for Hebrew. I will say this: I'm more upset than any of you.

The worst part was the dirt.

I never understood why they make the family shovel dirt onto you. What an awful thing. I appreciate you refused, Bessie. What's next? They make the kids push the embalming fluid into my veins? Honestly, the whole thing was degrading. I'd kill your uncles for how much dirt they shoveled. Your grandfather seemed calmed by the ritual of it. And I believed him when he told me, as he poured it onto the coffin, "I wish it was me, Bob. I wish it was me."

My *zayde,* my father's father, died at ninety-six. Older than me. He was drunk as a skunk! He went to temple that morning, drank his weight in the wine they had there—probably brought his own potato vodka, too. It could dissolve paint. Then he crossed the street and a bus hit him. *Bam.* Dead. What a way to go. When they crowded around his body, he was smiling. The bus driver says he smiled at him. Or at least that was my brother Georgie's story. The funeral was a party at the temple. Everyone got drunk and walked home and lived to tell the tale.

My coffin was perfect. Absolutely perfect! Although I could have done without the Jewish star. What am I? A Zionist? All of a sudden everyone becomes very religious on behalf of the deceased.

I never understood why your mother went to that kibbutz. She had just been accepted to Columbia School of Architecture, and she had a bad feeling about the whole thing and decided to travel to Europe. So she flew to Paris and stayed with her friend Claire, who was an au pair for a wealthy family, and she got bored almost immediately and she met a few Jewish kids who said they were going to Israel to live in a *commune* and pick strawberries and smoke drugs. Heaven. So she bought a ticket to Tel Aviv the next day. She stayed in some terrible international hostel and asked around and ended up getting on a bus to a banana farm in the north along the Sea of Galilee.

It wasn't the type of kibbutz where they all danced around in peasant blouses and banged the tambourine and sang songs. It was a tough camp where the kids worked outside all day and drank arrak all night until they passed out in the fields and woke up with frost in their hair. Your mother arrived, and the old man in the front office had blue numbers down his arm and he gave her a job peeling potatoes in the mess hall. Every morning she'd wake up at dawn and put on rubber boots and stand in a cold vat full of potatoes and water, peeling them one by one and tossing them into another vat. *Plunk.* And in the afternoons she rode a tractor up and down the banana fields and picked the bunches in the sun, and her hands grew calloused and turned so brown people at the markets would speak to her in Arabic.

To her, it was paradise. She didn't have to think about architecture school. She didn't have to plan. She didn't have to worry about the boyfriend at Brown who'd asked her to get married. She didn't have to do anything but peel potatoes and ride a tractor. It was the same every day, every night, for two months.

· · ·

She sliced her hand open one morning and ended up in the medical tent, and the woman who patched her up was kind and funny and smart, and by the time she finished stitching her wound your mother had decided to become a doctor. Just like that.

I knew she'd be flying back to New York by way of Paris, and in one of her letters she said she'd call on Labor Day when she got back to Claire's apartment. Labor Day came and I didn't hear from her. No call, no telex, nothing. I woke your grandfather up at four the next morning and I said, "Something is the matter with Robin." He told me not to worry. Ha! That's the last time he ever did that.

On a whim, I called the American Hospital of Paris. That's the family rule: if anything happens to you when you go abroad, you go straight to the American Hospital. Whatever it costs. So I called and I said, "Robin Bell's room please," and I'll never forget what I heard next: "Just a moment." The longest moment of my life. And the nurse picked up and brought your mother the phone, and she said, "Mom . . ." I hung up and hit your grandfather on the head.

Then I got my handbag.

I got in the car and drove it to Kennedy Airport. I left the car at the curb and walked up to the ticket counter and said, "One way to Charles de Gaulle," and they said, "Today's flight is completely full, but you can go tomorrow," and I said, "I need to go now." I took out my wallet and started counting out bills. I paid double, all in cash, and sat in the jump seat next to the stewardesses in the galley. I don't think I blinked the whole flight. I was by your mother's side in eight hours. She had viral encephalitis. It was in her spine. They said she might

part one

MY MOTHER

THE FRUIT OF THE VINE

MY MOTHER TAUGHT ME EXACTLY ONE THING and it's how to make brisket.

It doesn't take a genius.

The key is you just leave it alone. You put the side of beef in a large pot, pour in whatever—red wine, tomatoes from a can, some carrots cut up, a half an onion, a fistful of kosher salt, a potato for your grandfather—and let it sit on a very low flame. I'd pour in some water if it got too dry, but otherwise, it required very little effort. You could forget about it for the entire day and there it would be. Don't say I never taught you anything.

How you loved my brisket. You didn't care if it was tough. You loved the taste of the gristle on the edges and the char from the bottom of the pot. Before you came over to the house in Ardsley for Passover or break the fast or what have you, you knew there would be brisket. You'd talk about it like a fiend. "Is it time for brisket yet?" "Grandma, is there going to be enough brisket?" Always with the appetite. Your parents never made beef because of your father's cholesterol, so you were probably very anemic. You needed the blood running through you.

It's my mother's recipe, more or less. She wasn't religious, but she felt it was very important to have everyone over to the house in the Greenpoint neighborhood of Brooklyn on Friday nights for Shabbat dinner. There wouldn't always be beef, but there'd be liver or sweetbreads or tongue. If you stew it long enough, what's the difference?

My brothers were all grown up and out of the house, and every week she'd invite them with their wives and their children to her dining room table—the same table where we were all born. She'd preside over the whole thing. She'd stand up, bang her fist on the table, take one of my father's matchbooks from her apron pocket, and strike a match. You could hear a pin drop. She'd lean her enormous breasts over the table and light two long candles in their brass holders she brought from Russia and shake out the match.

Then she'd put a kitchen cloth over her head. Like a looming ghost, she'd very slowly lift her hands up in front of her eyes and chant with her head bowed, her hands lilting back and forth with the incantations.

"*Baruch ata Adonai, Eloheinu Melech ha-olam, asher kid'shanu b'mitzvo-sav*"—which was incorrect, it's *b'mitzvo-tav* with a *t* not -*sav* with an *s,* but that's how it was in the Yiddish pronunciation—"*vitzivanu l'hadlik ner shel Shabbos.*"

Then still under the cloth she'd say to my brother, "Georgie-zun, *vayne!*"

Georgie would wink at me and foist up a cup of wine, his

chest all puffed out. He'd mouth along dramatically like an opera singer, and I'd try not to laugh as she continued on in her trance.

"Baruch ata Adonai, Eloheinu Melech ha-olam, boreh p'ri hagafen."

Blessed are you, Adonai, for giving us the fruit of the vine.

Imagine calling a jug of my *zayde*'s forty-cent kosher wine "the fruit of the vine." Hardly.

Then she'd take the cloth off her head and fold it back up on the table, just as her mother had done before her, and hers before her, and hers before her, and so on. And there she'd stand, solemn as a statue, beholding all her creation.

· · ·

So decades later I'd have the family over for Seder and we'd all be at my house in Ardsley in our nice clothes under the crystal chandelier. I'd stand at the head of the table and everyone would shut up. I'd light the candles in the same brass holders and I'd blow out the match and put my cloth napkin over my head. I didn't say the prayers—I never really learned the words. But I hummed softly to myself and rocked back and forth under the veil. You asked me what I was saying. "Rose, Rose, Rose." My mother's name.

Bessie, you are the only daughter of an only daughter of an only daughter. The fruit of the vine.

MY MOTHER

My mother was always at the movies.

She was an enormous Russian immigrant in a falling-down house right by the shipyard in Greenpoint and her English wasn't great, but she'd find a nickel and go to the theater and sit in the dark all day.

In the summers she'd go for the air-conditioning. She'd watch the same movie over and over until the sun went down and you could breathe the air again. Then she'd come home and make dinner, humming the musical score. She'd sway from side to side in front of the stove—she wasn't graceful— but she would transport herself. I always knew when she'd

been at the movies that day, because she'd be ⌐
mood, everything heightened. She'd embrace my fat⌐
he walked in the door all covered in sweat and dirt from ⌐
picket line, swept up in the romance. *"A gut ovnt,* Samuel!"
Good evening, Samuel. He didn't know what hit him.

She *adored* Buster Keaton. She insisted he was Jewish. She
read the sections in the paper about the movie stars, the glam-
our. The women in their silk gowns and ermine boas. She'd
impersonate the way they talked, and she was a large, impos-
ing woman—she gave birth to five children on the dining room
table because she didn't want to ruin the bed linens—but she
carried herself with a certain air.

She'd tell me, "If you're having a rotten day, go buy yourself
an ice cream soda and a new hat."

And that's what I would do.

So my mother was at the movies and my father was always
on the picket line. Do you know why they call it Union Square?
It's where the Socialist union organizers would go and stand
on their soapboxes—real soapboxes—and scream about workers' rights. These were the days when you could die in a fire at
your factory job in the United States and no one would bat an
eye. My father didn't work, though. When we were desperate
and out of money, he'd paint houses. That's what was listed
on the census as his official profession: "House painter." Ha.
He was a professional complainer. A protester. And he peti-
tioned. He'd take the bus into Manhattan and sleep on the
steps of City Hall until someone would talk to him and look at
his petition or hear his rallying cry or read his list of demands
on behalf of other men. We always had people staying in our
house, sleeping on the floor. My mother could barely feed us

kids, and my father would come with four, five union men and they'd say, "What's for dinner, Mrs. Otis?" She'd always say, "You tell me!" But somehow there would always be food. There would be blankets. There'd be conversation that lasted all night. We got by.

It's no wonder my mother needed to get out of the house. She thought she was done with babies when she had me. She was forty years old. Can you believe it?

She didn't tell anyone she was pregnant with me until the very end, because she wasn't entirely sure I'd be alive. I was very quiet in the womb. My brothers were so loud I was just in there listening, already enamored with them.

When I was born, the twins Georgie and Leo washed me off in the sink. I was their pet.

. . .

I almost died once before.

I was a very little girl, ten years old. And I was in the hospital with meningitis. In those days, there wasn't much anyone could do. We waited it out. And all four of my brothers never left my side. They were all grown up. David and Jesse had children of their own, but they slept in the hallway and on the floor of the hospital in shifts. They were certain I'd die. My hearing had gone in my right ear, so they read to me on my left side. One day, Leo leaned over and he said, "Bobby, if you die, I'll kill you." And I laughed so hard I coughed up bile. But I heard him loud and clear. I went home a week later, on Purim. Every. Flat. Surface. Of. My. Bedroom. Was covered in haman- taschen. There must have been two hundred cookies. Apricot,

poppy seed, fig—all the best flavors. I cried and they cried, and we invited the neighborhood over and we ate.

Did you know my name wasn't supposed to be Barbara?

It should have been Gloria. The afternoon I was born, my mother said, "Georgie, go down to the Social Security office and register the baby. Gloria Otis." And Georgie didn't like that name—too Jewish. So he and Leo and Jesse and David talked, and they all went down to the grand building on Fulton Street and registered my birth: Barbara Dorothy Otis.

I belonged to them.

PHONE CALL, OCTOBER 2009

GRANDMOTHER: Bessie, is he Jewish?
  GRANDDAUGHTER: *Hello to you, too!*

Is he Jewish?
  He's not. He's from Maine. He's a WASP from Maine.

So he's a Christian.
  He's nonpracticing—I think he's an atheist. We haven't really gotten into it. He's actually taking a class on Buddhism.

Oh my god.
  Grandma, it's not important to me.

How long have you been going together? Your mother says a
month.
So you already have the whole story!

I want to hear it from the horse's mouth.
Now I'm a horse.

Don't get cute. You know he's probably never taken home a
Jewish girl before.
*He goes to Brown. He's done nothing but take home Jewish
girls for four years.*

Can I tell you a true story?
Why not.

In the history of our family, only one person has ever married
a non-Jew.
*Grandma, it has been one month and he's probably moving
to San Francisco after—*

Bessie. Listen to your grandmother.
I'm listening.

Only one person has ever married outside the religion. My
brother George. He had his heart broken by a miserable
woman, and so he joined the navy and was stationed all over
the world.
*I didn't know we had anyone in the navy in our
family!*

Don't get too excited—there wasn't any combat. So he came home and showed up on my mother's doorstep with a beautiful Portuguese woman who was pregnant. And do you know what my mother did? My mother from the shtetl?

I can't even possibly begin to imagine.

She took one look at her son and one look at the girl, and she gave her a big bear hug and said in English, "Welcome to my home."

So you're fine with Charlie.

What's his major?

Business?

Fine.

OUR FACES

Bessie, I've told you my mother didn't speak a word of English when she got to Brooklyn—on the census forms they wrote her language was "Jewish." Ha! She spoke Yiddish with my father but never in front of the children. So we didn't talk much. She'd call me *shayna punim*, "beautiful face," which made me laugh. I had *her* face.

This was before the adjustments I made in the 1980s.

She worked to erase her ethnic heritage, her shtetl. She would hold Shabbat and there'd be Hebrew and candles, but there was never any kosher this or kosher that. We ate what we could and we liked it. She shuddered at the Hassids in their wigs, and I turned my nose up at them, too.

I always detested my nose—I looked in the mirror and I saw Russia. I paid for your mother's nose and I paid for your "deviated septum." Ha. I held frozen peas on your black-and-blue eyes and the Russia melted out of you. I don't know if all the procedures I had were to erase the aging or the shtetl. A little of both, I suppose.

I look at my wedding picture and your grandfather hasn't changed, but I barely recognize myself.

PHONE CALL, 2010

GRANDMOTHER: You know, it's not really California.

[LONG PAUSE]

GRANDDAUGHTER: *I'm pretty sure it is.*

Well, I think you've got the wrong idea. I don't want you

going out there thinking it's going to be sunshine and palm trees and la-di-da.
I know.

If you want that, come to Palm Beach. Stay as long as you like!
I know.

I've never heard of a muggier place than San Francisco. Cold and muggy.
Well, it can't be as bad as Providence.

It's worse.
What?

What I'm saying—and nobody will tell you this but me—is that your hair is going to be frizzy. All of the time. You'll be beside yourself.
Well, if it becomes unbearable I can get a spray or something. Or a hat.

A serum. I've already FedExed you a serum.
Okay. Thanks.

You see? What would you do without me?
I have no idea!

Bessie?
Yes?

You'd be *gorgeous* if you went a little blonder.

GEORGIE AND LEO

My mother lived a very long life and she would have lived longer if it weren't for my brothers. First there was David, then Jesse, then the twins, Georgie and Leo. They tortured her—but what was she to do? "Four boys," the neighbors would say. "A blessing." She'd snort and say, "You want 'em? You take 'em."

She was married at eighteen and had David at nineteen, and then Jesse and then the twins shortly after that, and then me at nearly forty. Can you imagine? Georgie and Leo were teenagers when I was born. Never a break, even when she thought she had a break. As soon as I could walk, she sent me off with them. "Take the girl and get out of my house," she'd say. So they did. And oh, would they have fun.

They'd play stickball in the street and take turns changing my diaper on the sidewalk.

They taught me how to crawl by all standing on one end of the living room cheering and hollering while I lay helpless on my stomach on the rug.

They all competed to see whose name I'd say first. Georgie won. Leo swore it was only because he'd stand over my crib chanting his name over and over again until I cracked. He never forgave Georgie for his name being the one I said first.

In the summers, they'd take me to Coney Island to the ocean. They pooled their money and bought me a real swimming suit, but they would strip down to their undergarments and jump off the end of the dock. It was full of bodies in the summer, and everyone was so poor in those years after the market crash, nobody minded swimming with Jews. So they'd have their fun and swim up to girls. Georgie and Leo were identical twins,

and this was very convenient. Georgie would make a girl laugh and swim away, and Leo would pick up right where Georgie left off and quote a poem and lay on the charm. Together, they were a real catch. They'd be at it for hours until they got someone's address. They'd divvy up the girls depending on who liked which one the best. They always had girlfriends.

Meanwhile, I'd sit on the edge of the pier on the hot concrete looking at them having their fun and my skin would blister—I'm very fair, like you—and how I'd cry. "Please, please let me swim!" and they'd look at each other and say, "Bobby, you'll drown." And I'd say, "I don't care!"

But Leo had an idea. Leo always had an idea—he was the smarter one, almost as smart as he thought he was. He sweet-talked a woman into lending him her black rubber inner tube, and he found some rope and tied it to a post and said, "All right, Bob, hop on!" And so I did. Every day for a week I'd sit on an inner tube tied to the post, terrified, with the cold water making me numb below the waist while they swam around. I could have slipped through and nobody would have known, and that would have been it. But I never slipped. I owed it to them to stay afloat. I sat there for hours, bobbing on the water.

All of my brothers could read and write, and all of them went to college except for Georgie, who joined my father on the picket line as soon as he could. They were full-time protesters who were too angry at the whole world to get any kind of work. They protested anything—after the terrible factory fire they protested for workers' rights. It was always something.

But Georgie and Leo were very smart. They were always reading—it was a competitive sport. Leo memorized the U.S. Constitution, and Georgie would add up numbers in the phone book. Leo would quiz me, and I was a little girl—I hardly knew how to spell my own name—but he bullied me into reading the great books, and Georgie ran multiplication tables with me. They would show off to each other depending on how fast I learned their lessons. If I got poor marks in school, they wouldn't look at me. "They want the Jews to stay behind while they go off to great schools and become rich men." So every night I read until I was nearly unconscious, and Leo would come into the room I shared with my mother (my father came home late and slept on the living room floor) and he'd pat me on the head and blow out the gas lamp. "Good night, good night, don't let the monkeys bite." I don't know why it was funny but I'd laugh every time.

Leo followed in David's footsteps and set off to become a lawyer. Leo graduated from college with honors and went on to Fordham Law School. He was going to be a great litigator. And then right before his last semester of law school, he fell terribly ill.

He'd kill me if he knew that I'm telling you what I'm about to tell you. So would Georgie. My mother didn't know the story as long as she lived. She would have bludgeoned them both with a frying pan. But I knew. I watched the whole thing happen. I was eight years old.

Leo got sick in early January, and by the end of February he was near death. It was a stomach infection that spread throughout his whole body. Now, Leo was the great scholar, but Georgie wasn't dumb. He was a whiz with numbers and a fast learner when he wasn't getting drunk with my father and my *zayde*. So he sobered up, put on Leo's gray wool blazer, took three buses up to Fordham, and strode confidently into Leo's class and signed his twin brother's name into the attendance log. For weeks, he'd sit in lectures, take notes, and stay up all night reading and memorizing all the cases. When he was called upon by a professor, he'd drop his Brooklyn accent and use the same "goyish" voice he'd relentlessly mock Leo for using. He passed the final exam with flying colors, in Leo's name.

As for Leo—as the illness progressed, he became certain he'd die. He lay up in his bedroom with the curtains drawn, sipping broth and sleeping off his fevers. Every day he became skinnier. His eyes sunk and his skin turned yellow and his hair started falling out. When Purim came, I brought home a poppy seed hamantasch from the temple potluck and took it to his room. He looked at it and laughed and then coughed and winced, and blood came out of his mouth. I dropped the cookie on the floor and ran. I found my mother in the kitchen, scrubbing a pot. "Ma, is Leo going to die?" She didn't pause to think: "Leo is going to graduate."

Leo still hadn't recovered by graduation day in June, so Georgie put on the cap and gown and walked across the stage in front of thousands of people and received Leo's diploma. He brought it home and told everyone he'd been by the school and picked it up. Nobody had any idea what was really going on except for me. Not even Jesse or David.

Then, in a month, it was time to take the bar. The New York State Bar is notoriously tough. John Kennedy Jr. failed twice, which'll show you what pedigree can and can't buy. But it was near impossible—it still is. And Georgie went to Leo, who at this point after five months was skin and bones; they didn't look anything alike anymore. Georgie said, "Leo, I'm going to take the bar." Leo protested—he was sure Georgie would fail—and the boys got into a terrible fight. Leo barely had his strength back, but he almost knocked Georgie to the floor when he told him he'd signed Leo up for the exam. "You've been a lawyer for half a year and you think you can pass the bar?" And Georgie looked at him with a grin and said, "No, I *know* I can pass it." This was the one time in our lives Leo asked me for advice. I was eight years old—I'll never forget it. "Bob, what do I do?" I told him, "If you die, you may as well die a lawyer." He was very amused by that—he'd tell it back to me all the time for years. So Leo gave Georgie his blessing and Georgie sat for the bar.

He passed the first time.

Two months later, Leo was better and he opened a law practice. My mother never asked how.

A few years later, after I'd recovered from my own illness, I was deaf in my right ear and I was very upset. It was permanent. I was beside myself, and I refused to get out of bed one morning. My mother sent Leo to me. When he walked in I blurted out, "I'm an invalid! What am I going to do?" So he put his face very close to my face and looked me in the eye and he shouted, "Use the left one!" Oh, how I laughed.

TWO VOICE MAILS, DECEMBER 30, 2011

Oh, you're probably asleep—it's early. Can I tell you a true story? You know your mother was working full-time when she had you. She took a few weeks off, but she went right back to finish her psychiatric residency. There were hardly any women in the program—there wasn't any precedent. And of course your father was in the same boat, and there were scheduling issues. Your mother cried. And I was in Florida! So what was she going to do? Leave you with a stranger? Oh my god. You couldn't hold your head up. Hello? I have a call waiting.

[END OF MESSAGE. NEXT MESSAGE.]

So anyway, so I'd get on an airplane every Tuesday and fly to LaGuardia and turn around and fly back every Thursday, because I loved you. I wasn't young. I was an old lady! But I loved you. And I'd sit there in their terrible apartment by the hospital and I'd watch you. We'd watch TV, we talked, it was fine. Every week for the first year of your life. Can you imagine? You started talking at nine months. You said "hi."

[LONG PAUSE]

Bessie, no serious person moves to San Francisco.

NEIMAN MARCUS DRESSING ROOM, PALM BEACH, FLORIDA, 2010

GRANDMOTHER: Excuse me, miss! The two is too snug on her, we'll need a four!

SALESLADY: I'll be right back with a four!

GRANDDAUGHTER: *Grandma! Not everyone has to know.*

You'd be a two if it weren't a shift. You carry your weight in your hips like me.
I don't need a whole new dress for the wedding. I'll just wear the black one I wore to Rachel's.

No! It was too low cut.
I thought you liked that dress!

It wasn't right. You'll get a better one. Nobody will be wearing black at a daytime wedding.

SALESLADY: We have the four!

[HANDS OVER A PALE BLUE EYELET SHIFT DRESS]

My granddaughter wants to wear a black dress to a daytime wedding.

SALESLADY: Oh?

[STANDS IN SILENCE, UNSURE WHO HOLDS THE CARDS]

I'm just saying I have a black dress I know I like and I've only worn it once.

It's vulgar.

SALESLADY: We just got in some really pretty new prints from Diane von Furstenberg!

No! They're always cheap polyester year after year. She'll look like a secretary from Yonkers. Why should we all wrap ourselves in kitchen wallpaper just because Diane von Furstenberg married up and got handed a fashion label?

[EVERYONE STANDS IN SILENCE]

[A FEW MORE BEATS OF SILENCE]

Thanks. I'll try on the four.

If it doesn't fit I'll light my hair on fire.

[SALESLADY EXITS]

PHONE CALL, 2009

GRANDDAUGHTER: *Grandma, I'm going to Maine for Christmas to meet Charlie's family.*

GRANDMOTHER: To Maine?
That's where he grew up.

I thought you said he went to boarding school.
Right. Yes. But his family lived in Maine.

Well, they kicked him out.
They didn't kick him out! It's just how they do things. His whole family went to that boarding school.

Mm-hmm.
What?!

In this family, we don't send our children away.
It wasn't like that at all!

Bessie?
What, Grandma?

You will not send your children there no matter what Charlie says. There are plenty of good schools where you don't have to abandon your child.

Grandma, we've been dating for three months.

I know.

We don't even live together.

You will.

I don't know that.

I do.

Oh really? How do you know?

Because it's the middle of December and you're going to Maine.

THE MOTHERLAND

It was when I was ten years old and fighting for my life in that hospital bed with meningitis, when my mother told me about Russia and how she left. How she escaped.

We never spoke about it after that. I would see it in my dreams, though, for the rest of my life. I'd wake up certain I was there, in the crowded berth of a steamship, alone. If you must know, I'm fairly certain the only reason she told me about it all is she was sure I was going to die, and she had to make sure I knew the story before I crossed over and met her mother and father and all her brothers and her sisters. It's possible she resented that I lived, that I carried around her horror, reflecting it back at her across the dining room table, scared of the woman cooking me eggs.

People then didn't talk about the journey, Bessie. There wasn't any "sharing" between parents and their children. If I brought it up, she'd say, "What's the point?" or pretend she hadn't heard, humming a song to drown me out. I knew Russia was there—she wore it in her sunken eyes, her clenched jaw, and her heaving sighs when she lay down at night. She'd allude to it if I complained: "You don't know how lucky you are, Barbara." Shaming me for the life she gave me: "You have it so easy, Barbara." Accusing me of existing in my own circumstances. I knew what she meant, and I'd bite my lip.

When she told me the story, it was early morning, the light barely coming in through the hospital curtains. She had been sitting by my bedside all night.

She closed her eyes and leaned back in her chair. "Bubbeleh," she began, "let me tell you about when I was your age."

She talked about herself as a little girl in a town called Pinsk in Belarus. It was the 1880s, after the first pogrom, when the tsar sent his marauders into the shtetls to drag Jewish patriarchs out of their homes and shoot them in the streets, while their neighbors cowered with their gas lamps off, awaiting the same fate. She told me how after they'd killed the fathers, they'd arrested the sons on made-up charges and sent them to march in the front lines of the tsar's army. Cannon fodder. Then they'd raped the daughters and left the mothers beaten and babbling and afraid of the night, waiting for the clomping of the horses' hooves against the cobblestones again.

"That's how it was, that's how it is, that's how it always was,

that's how it always will be, Barbara," she said. "Every hundred years they find a new reason to hunt the Jews."

When my mother was born, her family had already been destroyed by the tsar's regime. She had a brother and a sister she loved, Chaim and Bertha. She had two brothers who were sent to fight for the tsar and never returned, Gedalia and Sholom. She had a baby sister, Beryl, whom she never met. She told me about them, but at this point in the story I could hardly pay attention, and I was thirsty and hot and there was a ringing in my right ear that wouldn't stop and I missed the whole part about her siblings. She never spoke about them again. Oh well. I'm sure they were all lovely people. And now they're as dead as I am.

She brought me some water and I perked up.

She told me how when she was very young, her father, Max Brazel—Brazel was her family name—would walk from the shtetl to the center market in Pinsk to rally labor organizers. How her mother, Sarah, slept in a chair by the window at night, waiting for her boys to come home. How her teachers taught them nothing but Yiddish and the Talmud, and how she memorized the stories of Abraham and Sarah and their children and told them to her mother to soothe her as they bathed together and braided each other's hair.

How she and her friends would walk to school past the kosher butcher opening his shop, his apron already pink, and he'd wave to the children and ask them to tell their mothers his prices couldn't be beat. How nobody did, because the taxes the Russian government put on kosher meat made it unaffordable. How all the children would return home to potatoes and brown gravy flavored with bread and salt, while shanks of good beef were rotting in the butcher's windows, turning for the flies.

How after the tsar's murder in the spring of 1881, there were rumors going around Belarus that the Jews had done it. How the revolution was a conspiracy. How there were whispers of another pogrom. How her father left for town one morning with a solemn face and did not return that night. How he did not return the next day. How, after that, every day felt like the day before a rainstorm was set to fall.

One night at dinner her mother looked at her across the table and said, "There is no life here, Rose. Only death." She told her mother they should go to America—the neighbor boy had called it the Goldene Medinah, the Promised Land, flowing with milk and honey. And her mother said, "I cannot go." And she put down her spoon and said, "You must go." There wasn't a discussion. It was an order.

There was a man, Otesky—her father knew him from a trip he took to Minsk. This man had taken his family to New York. Her father despised him for it; he called Otesky a traitor of the shtetl. A coward. Her father had spit at the name, but she privately remembered it, stored it away for safekeeping, chanting it under her breath as she fell asleep at night: "Otesky, Otesky, Otesky." She combed and braided her hair and put on her clean dress and went to a Jewish refugee organization's office and asked for sponsorship to New York. They refused—they wouldn't send a little girl all alone. They told her they just sponsored the "heads of households." She went outside and kicked the wall of the Jewish refugee organization so hard her toenail turned black in her boot.

She knew she'd have to raise the money herself and she came up with a plan. She followed the kosher milkman on his route through the shtetl until he agreed to let her tag along and sell rags. She tore pieces of cloth from her father's and brothers' old coats and pants and shirts and peddled them to the milkman's customers. She would give the milkman half her profits and put the rest in a jar under her bed. She did this for a year, tearing clothes to make rags and riding in the milkman's cart every morning before school, the kopecks and rubles jangling in her pocket.

On the day she had finally saved the equivalent of twenty American dollars, she packed a small satchel. It was just after her twelfth birthday, which nobody acknowledged. She took two brass Shabbat candlesticks she mistook for gold, a pair of wool socks, a shawl her mother had knit, and her boiled wool coat. She considered taking her cloth bunny rabbit; she picked it up and stared at it. She was too scared to kiss her mother goodbye, so she kissed the rabbit instead and left it on the bed.

She said she regretted kissing the rabbit instead of her mother every second of every day. She told me how every time she looked at her own children and let herself fill with love for them, she'd imagine them doing the same thing she did to her mother and feel the metallic bile rise to her mouth. She grew very quiet for a few minutes, and I started drifting off to sleep in my hospital bed.

She shook me awake and told me that the morning she left the shtetl, she waited outside her house for the milkman. He picked her up for their usual route, and she told him she would give him an extra few kopeks if he would drive her to the train station in Brest. He refused the money and instead handed her a bag with ten small tins of pickled herring. He'd been hauling it around for her for weeks. He told her all the food on the boat would be *trayf* and she'd starve. She said when he handed her the bag of tinned herring, she held it so tightly her fingernails dug into her palms and she bled.

The milkman gave her advice: "When you get to the border, find the other Jews. They will show you where to go. They will care for you. Find the other Jews." He repeated that to her and she repeated it to me, and for a few minutes I didn't know if she was the milkman or my mother and which Jews she was talking about, so I said it back to her. "I'll find the other Jews, Ma." She laughed at me and I laughed with her, and then she shushed me and kept going.

Then she began the story of the escape. In the fog of my

fever and the confusion and discomfort and pain, I envisioned it so clearly I thought of it as my story. And when I told it to your mother, she'd think of it as her story. And when she told it to you, you'd think of it as your story. It's her story, Bessie, but it belongs to us. When she stepped off the boat, we all became possible.

It started with the train. My mother took it all day from Brest to the Russian town on the Austrian border. The train came to a stop and she started to look around for Jewish faces, when an enormous bearded man walked the aisle and stopped over her seat and asked in Yiddish, "Jewish?" and she didn't know if her answer would kill her or save her, so she took a guess and nodded yes.

The man took her by the arm and brought her out of the train into the night, her satchel clenched to her chest. The man walked with her for hours. They walked for so long her toe bled in her shoe. She didn't look behind her; she just walked into the dark.

With the man, she crossed a checkpoint. Then she was left at a "forwarding house" full of Jewish families all making the same journey, eating their bread and kosher stew in silence. The woman who ran the house called my mother "filthy," and my mother narrowed her eyes and resolved not to be bothered by that word. Her filth marked how long she had survived, how improbable it was she had come this far.

In the morning my mother and two other girls traveling alone were taken out the back door of the forwarding house and loaded into the back of a horse-drawn potato cart. The cart bounced so violently over the cobblestones, one of her knees knocked out her rotten tooth and it bled all over her coat. After hours and hours of bumping and jostling, the girls were loaded into another house, where they were given new clothes and fresh milk. They woke up in the dark to an elderly man with a kind face and round golden spectacles standing over them saying, "The boat is in Hamburg."

He repeated "Hamburg" over and over again until my mother said it back. Then he smiled. He took my mother's money—all her money—and exchanged it for a currency she didn't recognize. Then he patted her on the head with pity, and she raised her chin and puffed out her chest and broadened her shoulders and showed him she was a serious woman. The man walked my mother and a Russian family to a train station and handed them tickets.

She told me all about the train to Hamburg. How all of Europe went by in the compartment window: thick forests, and cities with enormous and ornate buildings and factories, and endless farmland, white dots of sheep and cattle streaking by for hours. She fell asleep dreaming of milk and woke up to the sound of the girls shouting, "Hamburg! Hamburg!"

The train came to a stop by the port on a wide river she mistook for the ocean. From songs and stories her mother told her, she had learned the sea was blue and vast, but here it was dark green and smelled of rotten fish and burning coal. It occurred to her that her mother had never seen the ocean, and the thought, "If I'm turned away, I will go back to Pinsk and tell my mother the sea is green." She told me it was the first and last time she let herself think about her mother on the journey.

She got off the train and was immediately separated from the other girls, and the crowd pushed toward the chaos of the ticketing agents. She stood on her toes and handed the agent her twenty dollars and shouted, "New York," the first words she had ever spoken in English. She was handed a paper ticket she couldn't read, and the ticket agent pointed in the direction of a moving crowd, which she joined, her feet nearly lifting from the ground as she clutched her satchel to her chest, floating toward the docks with the throng.

Just before she boarded, a doctor combed through her hair and looked in her mouth and pulled open her coat and pulled down the sleeve of her dress and stabbed her arm with a needle as long as her hand. She told me she still had the scar, and she tapped her upper arm, which wobbled under her blouse.

She said after the inspection hucksters tried to sell her upgrades for her passage: a private berth, a special meal ticket. All fabrications. All predators. The milkman had warned her this very thing had happened to a man in the shtetl.

She said the ship was dark, hot, and crowded—the loudest place she'd ever been. The roar of the steam engines behind the walls, the voices bouncing off the metal all hours of the day and night. There were five people in her berth and only two cots. She said they'd sleep in shifts, and often she'd be too sick from the smell to fall asleep. The smell of the rotten meat stew served on planks in the middle of the sleeping quarters brined with the human stench of two hundred souls made her eyes water and her stomach turn. There was nowhere to wash. She relieved herself in a pot that was shared by the others in her berth. The days and nights felt like one long stretch of time.

She told me about a sailor who was "no good," who went into the berths at night, and her voice grew unsteady and she did not wish to discuss the sailor any further. She wiped the wet hair from my brow and stared at me for a long while before going on.

When the ship docked, she took her bag and left her coat, which was covered in sick. She said she had never smelled air as clean as New York's. Never felt air as warm as New York's. She waited for hours in line on the small island in the harbor, in the nervous hush of a thousand people praying to however many gods for the same fate. She remembered what the milkman had told her: "Don't rub your eye. Don't scratch your head. They'll send you back." She almost went blind in one eye because she held it open for too long forcing herself not to blink.

She stood in the hot crowd for hours and hours, until a man wrote down her name as best he could and stamped her through to the other side.

She told me how she had one word in pencil on a paper in her pocket: "Otesky."

How she had no idea that name had been changed on that island to the same name that she would later take by marriage and the name she would give me: "Otis."

How any of it could have happened, Bessie, is an absolute miracle. She said, "It was *beshert,* Barbara. It was meant to be." And here, a hundred and thirty years later, you are.

Your Hebrew name is Shoshanna, which means Rose. You're named for her in the tribe.

. . .

On the morning of my wedding it occurred to my mother she didn't have a pair of formal shoes.

My brother Leo had tried to give her money for some new clothes two whole weeks before the wedding, but she just laughed and called him a *nudnik*.

"You need a dress, Ma."

"I have two dresses."

"Come on. You need to look presentable in the photographs. They'll be in an album."

"All eyes will be on your Barbara."

That's what she called me to my brothers: "*Your* Barbara."

In all my life, I never saw my mother in a clothing store. She bought her shirts and skirts from a secondhand charity shop and mended them when they ripped and that was that. She was indifferent to her appearance—everything was sacrificed for us kids. She had disdain for the Italian family next door, with the matriarch in lipstick and a fur coat heading off to church every Sunday. "Who's it for, the Holy Ghost?"

When I was five years old, on the day of my brother David's law school graduation ceremony, she wore her brown skirt and her stained white blouse and her ratty old hat. On her way out the door she accidentally took my father's wool blazer, which was only about five and a half sizes too small for her. She barely noticed. The whole hour-and-a-half bus ride from Greenpoint to Morningside Heights, she sat there humming to herself, proud as anything you've ever seen, the circulation to her arms completely cut off.

Leo tried to say something. "Ma! You can hardly breathe in that thing."

"What does it matter?" She laughed. "Who cares about the fit of an old lady's coat?"

I have two words for you, Bessie: Giorgio Armani.

We got to Columbia, and I'll never forget the columns on the big white buildings and the curling bronze arches and the grandeur of it all. How the men walked around with such importance. Everyone in suits and ties and shiny shoes and carrying brown briefcases. I couldn't imagine anyone there had ever heard of Greenpoint. I imagined them going home to their enormous apartments with endless rooms and servants who bowed and curtsied at the door.

We filed onto benches set up on the great lawn and waited with the other families—cleaner, more comfortable families. They all seemed completely at ease, bored even, fanning themselves with their programs and dreaming about lunch.

My mother was humming to herself and staring straight ahead. I saw how she was sweating from her temples. I watched the sweat form rivulets in front of her ears, down her neck, pooling in her collar. Leo noticed, too. "Ma, for God's sake. Unbutton the jacket." She shushed him and sucked in her gut and straightened her back and jabbed him in the ribs.

We waited and we waited, and finally a man with a funny hat called out over the whole lawn, "David . . . Otis!"

She shot out of her seat and brought her fingers to her lips and whistled so loudly the family in front of us turned around and glared, and just as she applauded over her head, the damned jacket split under both arms. *Zzzzzzppppp.* Two huge tears, exposing the soaking wet blouse underneath for all of Columbia to see. I felt my face burn with a shame I had never experienced before.

But when I looked up at her, I held my tongue. She was beaming. I had never seen my mother smile like that before. I'd hardly seen her smile at all! Tears were streaming down her face as she clutched her hands together beneath her chin and repeated, "My son, my son, my son."

Up in the distance, there was David in his long flowing blue robe, walking across the stage toward the dean, waving out at all of us and at the woman who got on a ship when she was just a girl so that one day, decades later, she could watch her child shake the hand of a kingmaker.

. . .

So on the morning of my wedding, my mother wakes up and doesn't have any dress shoes.

I had already gone over to Leo's house down the block to prepare. His wonderful wife, Lily, had sewn my dress by hand. She took me to the Garment District and bought yards and yards of ivory satin, and she pinned it to her dress form and made the most beautiful gown. It was flowing with an enormous train.

And all of that was happening and my mother was standing there in front of her wardrobe. And it's a Sunday and nothing is open but the hardware store. So she walks in and buys a can of black paint and a paintbrush. She brought them home and lined the front stoop with newspaper. She took her brown work boots outside to the stoop and painted them black. Three coats, carefully applied.

The people walking by on their way to church must've thought she'd lost her mind. "Oh, there's Mrs. Otis destroying some shoes. Hiya, Mrs. Otis!" She didn't care. She fanned them dry, put them on, laced them up, and made her way to the temple an hour early.

When the wedding was over the rabbi's secretary sent my father a cleaning bill for the synagogue carpet.

On the invoice it said, "Black footprints going up and down the aisle."

VOICE MAIL, 2012

Bessie, if you try on a dress and you don't immediately want to parade outside the dressing room and show it off to everyone in the store, take it off and forget it ever existed.

YOUR GRANDFATHER

I left Brooklyn when I was eighteen and I made it all the way to Manhattan.

I got into Hunter College, which in those days was all women. Georgie was so proud he took a taxicab to come visit after my first day. It must have cost him ten dollars, which in those days was a small fortune. He was leaning on the car outside the main building when I got out of class. He was dressed up: a three-piece suit and a hat. "My baby sister, the college student. I had to see it with my own eyes." Then he kissed me on the cheek, hit the hood, and got back in. A character.

Two years in, I met your grandfather.

It was on a city bus of all places. I had homework on my lap—math. And out of the corner of my eye, this young man in a fraternity sweater and old shoes was inching closer and closer to me, which at first I assumed was a come-on. But he wasn't looking at me; he was looking over my shoulder at the homework, the equations. He was *peering*. The bus was crowded, but I felt his eyes on my paper like darts. So what did I do? I started to intentionally mix up the numbers, flubbing the answers. In reality I was a whiz at math—my brothers made sure of it—but with this man hovering over me, breathing down my neck, I'd add a zero or start to write down the correct answer and cross it out and put the wrong one in. And I did it in big, bold penmanship. To this day—hand to God—he doesn't have any idea.

So of course, your grandfather gets on his high horse and he sings out, "Wrong!" Can you believe it? Seventy years and it started with "Wrong!" So I turned my head and really laid it on thick: "Excuse me. I don't appreciate strange men criticizing me on the bus." And he laughed and said, "I ain't criticizing. I'm simply stating a fact." He really said "ain't." A Jewish kid, talking like a country bumpkin. And in that split second, I don't know what it was about his round face with that smirk in his eye—the bluest eye I'd ever seen—but I made a decision. I moved over two seats and slammed my notebook on the empty seat and handed him the pencil. "You want to do someone else's homework so badly, be my guest."

He stuck out his hand. "Hank Bell. City College. Engineering."

I shook it once. "Bobby Otis. Hunter College. Math."

Three years later, we were eating cherries jubilee at our wedding dinner.

.   .   .

So I met your grandfather on the bus and we were going together by the next day. He pulled up to my parents' house on West Street in an old jalopy—a station wagon he borrowed from a friend. It was to be our first date. So he got out of the car, introduced himself to my mother (she didn't say a word), and I left the house with him. I wore my fake pearls Georgie had gotten me when I was admitted to college. I felt very important getting into a car: your grandfather walked with his chest all puffed out, and he opened the door for me and held my hand when I got in.

He sat down in the driver's seat, proud as can be, but when he turned the key, there was a terrible, low rumbling sound and then a pop. He tried it again and the engine revved up, but then there was nothing. A dead engine. We sat there in silence and the color went out of his face. Before a second could go by, I threw my head back and I laughed until I cried. He was very sore about it at first and kept turning the key, until he gave

up and he laughed, too. And when he laughed his whole face turned into a great, big smile and I could feel my heart in my throat over the sight of him. I knew I'd do anything for that smile—the way his eyes disappeared, swallowed by his cheeks, and his shoulders shook and his breath caught in his chest. If I could see one thing for the rest of eternity, it would be your grandfather laughing.

But we were in the dead car and I was hungry. And enough was enough. So I marched him right back into the house and shouted up the stairs, and my brother Leo drove us to our first date. We went to a Jewish deli and we both ate liver sandwiches as big as your head, and for dessert I had an egg cream. That car must have sat outside my house for a week until someone carted it away.

I know I've told you a thousand times that after I graduated from college he proposed with a dinky ring from Woolworth's.

Wedding Reception and Dinner

in honor of

Mr. and Mrs. Harold K. Bell

Saturday, the Eleventh of December
Nineteen hundred and forty-eight

Ocean Parkway Jewish Center

... *Menu* ...

Hors d'Oeuvres Varies

Pineapple Surprise

Ripe and Green Olives   Hearts of Celery

Salted Nuts

Braised Sweetbreads, Pattie Shells
Mushroom Sauce

Vegetable Julienne

Roast Indiana Broiler

Rose Apple   Fresh Asparagus

Sweet Potato Puff

Mixed Green Salad, French Dressing

Hot Cherry Jubilee
Desert Glace

Petit Fours   Cookies

Demi Tasse

Pale Dry   Club Soda

Mints

———

VICTOR MAYER, Caterer

There was a notch carved into it to look like a diamond in the light. He had tears in his eyes and so did I. You've never heard anyone say yes louder.

But my father wouldn't hear of it. He didn't like the kid with the broken-down car and no prospects. He was a socialist until it came to the possibility of his daughter growing old under his roof. I desperately wanted to be married to your grandfather, and one morning, I looked at him and said, "I want to be your wife today," so we went down to the marriage bureau and I bought three pennies' worth of baby's breath from a corner store near the courthouse and we eloped. We didn't tell a soul. But every night, your grandfather would tell me, "Good night, Mrs. Bell. And if I don't see you again, good morning, Mrs. Bell."

Thank you for your
lovely gift and
kind wishes.

A couple years later we had our big wedding with all our family there. I wore the white dress, and as I walked down the aisle I winked at him under my veil. He winked back. He toasted me with sparkling cider at the reception in the temple: "To the love of my life. May she always get what she wants, whether I like it or not."

PHONE CALL, 2011

GRANDMOTHER: Bessie, everything you wear is black.
  GRANDDAUGHTER: *That's not true! That's not even remotely true!*

You wore black to Rachel's wedding.
So?

So you looked like you were in mourning. It was a summer wedding.
I like that dress.

Never mind what you like—would it *kill* you to wear some *color* every once in a while? Blue? Pink? Even a very pale pink. That would be a start. What they're wearing lately is *neons.*
What who's wearing?

All the girls.
All the girls?

Why *yes.* And in the style section. Neon handbags, neon belts, neon cardigans. You name it!
Well, I don't really like the sound of that.

Why don't you take down my credit card number and go to Bloomingdale's and buy yourself some nice things that aren't morose.
Ha. Why don't you tell me what you really think?

[NO PAUSE. NOT EVEN A BREATH.]

You should be engaged by this time next year.

VOICE MAIL, APRIL 3, 2011

Bessie, if you ever finally find a lipstick that actually, certifiably looks good on you, buy twenty of them. If it gets discontinued—and it always does—you'll never forgive yourself. Ever. Don't say I didn't warn you. [BEAT] Do they have a Bloomingdale's in San Francisco? Is it very small?

THE CHAIR THAT WOBBLED

Did I ever tell you how your grandfather made his money? The only reason I didn't die penniless is one day in 1950 a chair wobbled on a sidewalk.

I swear on your life every word of this is true.

When your grandfather and I got married, we moved into the apartment upstairs in my parents' house in Greenpoint. "Apartment" is a generous word for what it was: An attic. A space under the eaves. There were two rooms separated by a wall that didn't reach the ceiling—one with a stove, one with a bed. The only running water in the building was on the ground floor, and so if God forbid I had to take a shower, I'd have to walk up two flights of stairs in a towel past all my relatives.

Up in the attic your grandfather would chase mice around with a broomstick, and when it rained we'd leave a tin pot on the floor and all night we'd hear *plunk plunk plunk*.

We'd both graduated from college and your grandfather was taking jobs as an accountant and making almost no money,

and there was very little I could do to change our situation drastically.

In those days, I had three options: I could be a secretary or a teacher or a nurse—you put on a skirt and looked after other people's problems while yours stayed the same. No thank you. I refused to be at the beck and call of a man I didn't know, so I couldn't be a secretary. I didn't want to be a teacher because I couldn't bear the thought of wiping snot off noses all day. And I saw what nurses had to contend with once and that was enough. So I was out of options.

But your grandfather had something: He wasn't stupid. And

he was a born salesman. Some people—sometimes even you, Bessie—would call him a shyster. I call him resourceful.

He'd been doing it since he was in britches. When he was growing up in Brooklyn, his father owned a penny candy store on Amsterdam Avenue on the Upper West Side of Manhattan. It was a ritzy area, right near the Museum of Natural History, and when he was a little boy he'd leave school an hour early and ride the bus all the way uptown and plant himself outside his father's store with a big, swirly lollipop. And when the rich kids from Collegiate School and Trinity and Dwight and all the rest would walk past with their uniforms, knapsacks, and au pairs, he'd start the performance of a lifetime, taking big licks of the thing while crying out, "My oh my, this is de-licious!" and "Gee, I'm glad I spent a nickel here!"

The store did fine until his father dropped dead of a heart attack at forty-five.

But now it was 1950 and your grandfather was making forty dollars a week as an accountant for a builder, which was barely enough to survive. And I was pregnant. And I was tired of chasing mice with broomsticks and wearing his dungarees to the store in the winter because all my stockings had ripped. I'd had enough. And there was one thing I could do about it: nudge. Remember, you can always nudge.

One night when we were huddled around our kitchen table in the attic and the wind was hammering the walls and rattling the windows, one of the glass panes shattered in its frame—it just exploded. I didn't know if we were being shot at or bombed or *what*. There was glass on the floor, and now the wind was whipping into the room, and I stood up and I threw my hands in the air and I said, "Hank! You know how to make money for other people. It's time you make it for us. You need to go into business on your own." And he said, "I'd need to get an office and find a bookkeeper." And I said, "You're standing in your office and you're looking at your bookkeeper." And that was that.

He spent about a month reading through tax codes and real estate listings for tracts of land until he had an idea. He found something very interesting in the GI Bill: develop land and build houses exclusively for veterans, and you'd get an enormous tax abatement if you structured the bank loan correctly. Bessie, when I first explained this to you, you called it a loophole. Your grandfather called it an exciting opportunity. He was too young to fight in the war—he was all set to use his engineering degree to build fighter planes, but by the time he graduated from college, it had been over for years. So this was his way of helping. The returning soldiers needed good-quality, affordable housing, and he needed to get his pregnant wife out of the attic.

So he called up his friend Buzzy, who was a construction supervisor in the firm, and he said, "You know the job from the outside, I know the job from the inside—what do you say we sell houses on our own?" Buzzy agreed on the spot. And they pooled everything they had and they took out an ad in *The New York Times*: "Two Honest Young Jewish Builders Looking for Capital." Ha. They weren't builders at all. They were a kid with a hard hat and a kid with an adding machine. It wasn't a lie, exactly. Call it sleight of hand.

In any event, in two weeks they'd raised enough start-up investment, and your grandfather went to the bank and got a loan and he was off to become the honest young builder he advertised.

He found some cheap, low-lying land out on the Long Island Expressway. It wasn't exactly a swamp—he'll swear up and down it wasn't a swamp—but it was soggy here and there. It was wet. It can be argued that there was a stream running under it. But it was cheap, and there was a lot of it. It passed inspection by the Veterans Administration and your grandfather and Buzzy broke ground.

In those days, suburban developments were cropping up all over Westchester and Long Island, and your grandfather needed to find a way to make his stand out. By the time construction was finished it was the middle of June. And it was hotter than hell. There were headlines in the paper every other day about the record-breaking heat. "Ten Dead in Boynton Beach," like that.

And that gave your grandfather an idea. On July 4, he went into debt buying a second ad in *The New York Times*. There was a schematic of one of the houses and the location on a map and in huge lettering: WE! HAVE! AIR-CONDITIONING!

Only one of the units—the all-furnished staged unit—actually had an air conditioner. He had Buzzy install it by hand; there wasn't a company that was doing that at the time. When people got to the development, they were told they could buy an air-conditioned unit for a $700 surcharge or the base model with a free fan. Your grandfather sold out in forty-eight hours. The only unit that didn't sell was the one with the air-conditioning. Not one person wanted it in the end. But it got them in their cars.

What? Oh, please. Like you wouldn't have done the same.

When your grandfather came home from the final closing, he walked into my parents' living room with a leather briefcase.

"Bobby, get down here! Rose! Sam! *Zayde!* Everyone!"

His eyes were wild, crackling with electricity, and his cheeks were flushed.

We all gathered around him, and he put the briefcase on the cedar trunk we used as a coffee table and he started to giggle like a little kid.

"Have any of you ever heard of snow in July?"

He opened the briefcase and took out two big stacks of cash and threw them up in the air. And he walked through the falling paper bills and scooped me up in his arms and gave me a kiss on the mouth so hard my *zayde* waved his jug and cheered. That really happened. It sounds like a story, but it's absolutely true. He threw the money in the air and my *zayde* danced.

As the bills were falling all around us, my mother looked right at me and then rolled her eyes melodramatically. Rose Otis. The Buster Keaton of Belarus.

The summer went by and the houses were all sold and your grandfather was already looking to develop his next plot of land, when one morning at the end of August the whole house was awoken at dawn by a phone call.

It was a woman in one of the houses. She was in hysterics. Your grandfather had handed all the homeowners a business card with my parents' phone number on it, and he told them if there was ever any trouble with anything, he would personally come and fix it. Nobody called—they were all too proud, or maybe they knew enough not to trust your grandfather with a wrench.

But this woman was furious. She was screaming. She said she woke up to let her little dog out and there were geysers in the middle of her lawn. Two fountains shooting up from the grass. "My house is sinking!" She screamed so loud I could hear it coming out of the receiver from across the room. "You sold me a sinking house! I'm calling the newspaper!"

"Calm down, calm down, it'll be all right. It's just been a rainy month." Your grandfather was snapping his fingers for his pants and shoes. I ran them to him, and he got dressed still on the phone with the woman. "I'll be there in an hour."

And your grandfather got into his station wagon, and I handed the baby to my *zayde* and ran out of the house and got in the car next to him.

"Where do you think you're going?"

"Do you really want to handle a screaming woman on your own?"

"This doesn't concern you, Bob."

"Like hell it doesn't."

He said nothing, and we drove in the early gray light all the way to Long Island. He was gripping the steering wheel so hard I thought it would break off.

By the time we arrived at the house, there was a photographer and a reporter outside.

"Harold Bell? Are you Harold Bell?"

"That's me!"

"Will you refund Mr. and Mrs. Lipowitz for their sinking house?"

I grabbed your grandfather's arm and said, "There aren't any sinking houses and there won't be any refunds."

Your grandfather went in the house and the Lipowitzes

were standing there around a chair in the living room, fuming. Your grandfather—I could kill him—opened with a joke:

"For a sinking house, you people look awfully dry."

Mrs. Lipowitz wasn't having any of it. She looked like she was about to knock him flat on his back. I chimed right in.

"I'm Hank's wife, Bobby Bell."

She softened a little. "Suzanne."

"I had a sorority sister called Suzanne. Wonderful girl. A brunette just like you."

"You look familiar. Did you go to Bryn Mawr?"

"No, Hunter. I just have one of those Jewish faces."

"Don't we all!"

There was a moment of silence, and then we were just two gals laughing.

But her husband was still irate. He pointed at the chair in the middle of the floor. "This chair wobbles."

Your grandfather crossed his arms. "Excuse me?"

"Go ahead. Sit in the chair. The whole house is uneven."

I didn't say a word, but I gave your grandfather a look that said, "If you sit in that chair your whole life will be over."

Your grandfather walked over to the chair, held the back of it, and gave it a shake. "The floor's fine. The chair's uneven."

"No, it's not. It's part of a set."

"What does being part of a set have anything to do with it?"

The two men stared at each other. The reporter was outside with the photographer. Your grandfather had an idea. A gamble. He picked up the chair and walked out the door with it. We all followed him. The reporter sprang into action and the photographer readied himself.

Your grandfather took the chair all the way to the sidewalk

and held it up as he shouted at the small crowd. "They say the house is uneven. They say the chair is proof. I'm here to tell you, this is a case of a wobbly chair, not a sinking house."

He set the chair down and gestured to it grandly.

"Mrs. Lipowitz, will you do me the honor of having a seat?"

The woman trudged over to the chair and sat down.

Ka-klunk.

It wobbled.

And we got in our car and drove home.

You enjoyed your private high school? Your college tuition? Thank the chair.

But let me be perfectly clear about something: all those houses are still standing. Hank made sure they were all retro-fitted. There's nothing wrong with them. Except every few years when the Long Island Sound floods, the groundwater rises up in the front yards and there are ducks swimming around people's mailboxes.

. . .

Eventually, your grandfather grew tired of selling Levittowns. He'd sold hundreds of them. A development with fifty houses one weekend, forty houses another. Each house selling for anywhere from $20,000 to $80,000. He was printing money. And he grew bored immediately. He needed a new market, a new challenge, with less hassle. He left Buzzy the Long Island developments and he went off on his own.

There was another way to build—cheaper houses, but better quality—without paying the Mafia a cut for the labor, which is how construction worked back then. They called it "prefabrication." Prefab. The idea was all the pieces were made in a factory ahead of time and shipped to the job site. There was very little overhead, and buildings could go up fast.

In those days, only the Russians were doing prefabrication. It was considered Soviet technology. Your grandfather read about it and he found the whole thing marvelous. "Bobby, they make an entire floor of a building in a day. They make rooms in a factory—with the wires and pipes and everything."

"That's wonderful, Hank."

It all honestly sounded like science fiction. But your grandfather was determined. And he found a way to do it. In the 1960s the Department of Housing and Urban Development gave out twenty-two grants nationally to support prefabricated housing to help families move into affordable homes.

Your grandfather got one of the grants. So he went to Russia on a diplomatic mission to study postwar building technology. That's what the official cover was. "Diplomatic missions." He'd go and talk to their ministers of housing and walk through their factories, and when he returned to the States he'd be debriefed for hours and all his luggage would be combed through by a man in white gloves. He must have gone to Russia ten times throughout the 1960s and '70s.

Your mother once asked him if he was a spy, and he winked at her and said, "Robbie, I could tell you, but I'd have to kill you," and she burst out crying. I hit him over the head with my newspaper.

After his very first trip to Russia, he came back to the States and used the grant money to buy a factory along the East River in the north Bronx, and he hired a nonunion crew and paid them a union wage, full benefits. He went into the local community, which was very poor and suffered from terrible unemployment, and passed around flyers at churches and popular restaurants. By the time the factory was up and running, he had hired an almost completely local crew. He didn't bus in labor; he wanted the community to profit. Not just the assembly-line workers—the foreman, the accountant, the secretary in the front office. The whole factory was run by people who lived nearby in Fordham Heights.

By the next summer, he had a billboard on the Cross Bronx Expressway of a happy family swimming and lounging around a turquoise swimming pool with a gray tower looming over it. LIVE SWIMMINGLY! Nobody will tell you he isn't a born salesman. Every unit was sold by the time the final story was laid in place by an enormous crane.

He had learned his lesson from the houses he built accidentally on a swamp. These new apartments were perfect. He wanted to be an engineer. He could tell you about drying temperatures to make the concrete lighter but strong enough to bear weight. He had his notes from eight different Soviet factories and combined the technology to maximize the quality of the materials, the durability of the buildings. They required very little maintenance. They were affordable, too, but they were solid.

To this day that first project is the tallest prefabricated residential building in Westchester County. Your grandfather mentions that to you only about thirty times a year.

There's only one other building that makes him more proud: his tree house. It was 1965 and the whole country was panicked about the possibility of a nuclear missile. Our neighbor in Ardsley dug an enormous hole in his backyard and poured in a concrete shell. He brought in pallets of canned soup and an oxygen tank and sleeping bags. A fallout shelter. It frightened me. I asked your grandfather, "Hank, should we build a bunker?" He said, "I'll do you one better." That weekend, he brought in lumber and a cherry picker, and he built an enormous tree house in the elm tree right on our property line with the doomsday neighbor. When it was done on Sunday night, he brought me up the ladder. There was a table and chairs, a white tablecloth, and a bottle of champagne and two crystal glasses. "Bobby, when the bomb hits, here's where I want to be. Up in the sky with you." We spent the better part of that night in the tree house.

So they completed the prefabricated tower and started making smaller apartment buildings, and suddenly hundreds of families who lived all cramped in unsafe conditions could afford three bedrooms in a good school district out of the city. He sold the apartments to any factory workers who wanted them at a discount. The community in Fordham Heights was thrilled and the new homeowners were thrilled and I was thrilled.

Everything was hunky-dory until the Mafia got involved.

In those days, the Mob controlled construction because they controlled the unions. And your grandfather had created a building technology that made those union workers obsolete. And so one day, two men showed up to the factory in a black sedan and asked for your grandfather by name and found him in his office kibitzing with the workers, and they cleared the room and told your grandfather he had to close the factory. They didn't ask him. They told him.

Your grandfather knew why they were there. So he asked them, "How much do you take from the unions per job?" And

Peter wanted to get your grandfather's ideas about fighting Columbia's plan to take over a residential area of Harlem to build an enormous athletic complex and Olympic-sized swimming pool. It would have displaced the residents completely and been off-limits to the community that remained. Terrible. Peter needed someone smart to go up against the board. Someone who understood laws around affordable housing. To prevent Columbia from becoming a predatory slumlord.

Your grandfather knew eminent domain law backward and forward, and he came in and drafted a plan to protect the housing projects around Columbia. He won. He defeated the board. And as a reward, Peter got him hired. Columbia gave him a faculty position in the department of urban planning. Your grandfather developed a course about the building business: Real Estate Entrepreneurialism for Architects, Builders, Developers, Buyers & Sellers. He taught the kids all his tricks.

The board tried every way to toss him out. And they would have succeeded if the Students for a Democratic Society didn't rise up and take over the administration building in the spring of 1968. The SDS kids loved your grandfather because to them he was a Russian socialist who fought on behalf of Harlem, and they named your grandfather the faculty representative. The SDS headquarters during the student occupation was in the Columbia School of Architecture. In your grandfather's office.

When you were a little girl, your grandfather took you to his office and pointed out a faint mark on the white marble staircase in the building lobby. He had you kneel down and squint. You barely saw anything, but you humored him. "What is it?"

"That's the blood from the back of my head when the

university police dragged me out the door during one of the protests."

"Why did they drag you?"

"Because I didn't want to go!"

Stubborn. For the greater good. To get us out of the attic.

At ninety-one he still teaches his class at Columbia every Tuesday morning in the fall semester. He loves the students. Loves challenging them. Fighting with them. Pushing them to find new technologies to solve problems. During his office hours, if a student asks him how he went into business, his eyes will glimmer and he'll smirk and he'll lean forward in his chair and say, "Let me tell you a true story about a chair that wobbled."

ESTELLE

I had one other great love aside from your grandfather. Estelle. My dearest friend.

Estelle was my sorority sister, and we were very close until the day she died far too young at seventy-two.

We were two Jewish girls from Brooklyn at Hunter College, and she had grown up very, very poor. The whole family on a mattress in a one-room apartment, scraping by for food. Her father was very ill and one of her siblings was always near death, and her mother worked as a cleaner or whatever else she could find for work. Estelle was brilliant. When she was a young girl she sat down at a piano in a bar and could play it. She sang for money. She saved it all. She never missed a day of

school and read books like a maniac. She learned French from an Algerian coffee man and spoke it fluently. She read at the dinner table. She read walking. She once tripped over a garbage can and got a scar on her forehead, which never healed properly. That really happened, I swear on your life.

When I first saw her, she was sitting on a bench in a hallway outside a sorority mixer, reading.

"Mind if I join you?"

She scooted over without looking up. I watched people file by and waited until she finished her chapter.

"Bobby Bell. I think we're going to get along."

She looked over at me and smiled and shook my hand, her long black curls swept to one side and her eyes glinting blue gray like a wolf. She was the most beautiful person I had ever seen in my entire life. Everybody agreed.

She met Albert around the same time I met your grand-father. The two men hated each other. Your grandfather was smart and could look right through a person. Albert was a big pear-shaped man with a temper, and he was already a drunk. But he was training to be a doctor—a urologist, which was a very good specialty. He came from money—Jewish money; his parents were Austrian diamond dealers and they owned a brownstone on the Upper West Side of Manhattan. And he was infatuated with Estelle. He waited for her after class, he waited outside the sorority house, he would show up in the middle of the night and stand in the street singing, *"Estelle, Estelle, I'm livin' in hell, wake up, my belle, Estelle, Estelle."*

I told you she was very poor. In those days, you didn't marry up, you married out. So she did. The second she graduated. And they moved to a big white colonial house in Mount Vernon with these stupid columns. Estelle got her teaching certificate and taught French at the high school there, which she adored. She couldn't carry a child for many years, and Albert grew impatient with her. I told you he had a temper. We didn't have the term for it then. He was *severe*. She would call up my mother's house—your grandfather and I were still living in the attic with your uncle—and she'd be whispering and often hang up abruptly, *click*. I'd get a call back in an hour and her voice would be flat and she'd apologize for nothing.

When I got pregnant with your mother, she conceived Nancy. Your grandfather and I bought the house in Ardsley, which was even nicer than Mount Vernon—better schools—and Estelle and I would meet up at each other's kitchen tables and drink tea and smoke cigarettes and just chat. We didn't talk about Albert, we didn't talk about the babies we were car-

rying; we just gossiped about the horrible people in our neigh-
borhoods and the dumb housewives, and then we'd read the
paper and smoke some more. Nancy and your mother were
born a month apart in December and January—two winter
babies.

Estelle and Nancy were very bonded; she protected her.
She taught her constantly. I didn't know your mother could
read until she pointed to my Sears catalogue and said, "'Now
in *red*!'" Nancy and your mother got along—they didn't have a
choice, really. Robin knew there was something off about Nancy's house. She'd talk about being scared of Nancy's father—
that he'd take things out of Nancy's hands. She kept saying,
"He takes things from her." Who knows.

I'll never forget the afternoon in the kitchen in Ardsley
when Nancy and your mother were around five years of age.
Estelle had driven Nancy to the house that morning. They
were two little girls giggling at the table, talking their heads
off. Estelle and I were cleaning up lunch dishes when I looked
over. She was just standing there, her back toward everyone,
straight as a rod, not moving with the water filling up the sink.
The girls were just a few feet away, in their own world, and
there she was, tears streaming down her face. I turned off
the tap and I held her hand in mine, and we just stood there
together taking deep breaths.

We never talked about it after that. That's just how it was.

When Nancy graduated from Barnard, she joined the Hare
Krishnas and cut off her hair. It lasted only a few years before
she came to her senses and married an estate lawyer, but for
her early twenties she wore the robes and everything. Estelle
was beside herself. What could she do? So I told her: "You go

to Paris." She made an arrangement with Albert: For half the year, she'd live in the house in Mount Vernon. The other half of the year, she'd teach English in Paris. He bought her a small apartment on the Left Bank, and she'd go there and get big and fat and happy and read great books in French and have the time of her life. And then she'd wither up in Westchester in the summers, and then she'd go back, and she did that for over a decade until she died of a heart attack coming off the plane in Newark Airport. There was duck liver wrapped in tinfoil hidden in her suitcase.

BREAKFAST, PALM BEACH

GRANDMOTHER: Did you know I marched on Washington with Martin Luther King?
GRANDDAUGHTER: *I didn't!*

I took the bus down from White Plains alone—your grandfather threw a *kinipchin* fit about that.
About what?

About how I took a bus ride to Washington by myself. In the dead of night.
GRANDFATHER: What do I care if you took the bus? It's a miracle you got on a bus.

Well, I was traveling alone as a very attractive young girl.
GRANDFATHER: This is true. I grant you that.

And so I got there and walked straight to the Washington Monument, and I marched. I marched arm in arm with perfect strangers. And I kept at it until I fainted.

GRANDFATHER: You didn't faint.

I came very close.

GRANDFATHER: Bull!

I kept at it through a pouring rainstorm.

GRANDFATHER: A monsoon, I'm sure.

It was a rainstorm and I can prove it.

[REGARDS THE OCEAN OUT THE WINDOW]

I had a beautiful green alligator handbag—what I thought was an alligator handbag—and I was out on the Capitol steps and I looked down and all down the front of my khaki trench coat was *green* ink. A green mess. Awful! Can you imagine?

GRANDDAUGHTER: *Well, no.*

There are two lessons here, Bessie.

Okay.

No matter what happens, keep walking. My *zayde* always said that if the earth is cracking behind you right up to your heels, you put one foot in front of the other. You keep going. Nothing's as important as moving forward.

What's the second lesson?

Never. Buy. Fake. Anything.

TWO DAYS DEAD

When I die you'll have two days to kill before you have to get to Martha's Vineyard for the burial. You still won't be good at crying in front of Charlie—he's a WASP, they don't do histrionics. That will be your assumption anyway. He would've loved for you to let him see you hurt. You were trying to protect him, trying to make your pain invisible. Without a witness. It's just noises into a pillow.

You'll do something very strange the day after you get the call. You'll get out of the house and go to Koreatown to the women-only spa. You'd gone there twice before, once with your friend the lawyer and once by yourself after a bad day at work. You'll get in the car and drive yourself (terrible!) and pay the woman twenty dollars. She'll ask if you have an appointment, and you'll say, "No, I don't have an appointment." It will be the first full sentence you spoke that day. You'll make an appointment for a manicure. A manicure! You'll think, "I shouldn't have chipped nails for the funeral." My granddaughter. It wouldn't have mattered.

You'll change into the thin cotton robe in a shade of green that will make you look very peaked. You'll take your towel to the showers in a trance. You'll make yourself very clean, you'll get shampoo in your eye, and the tears will start again. You'll sit in the tub naked and, like a child in a bath, you'll watch your arms float, in disbelief at how pleasant it all is. You'll look around at the bodies in the room, a parade of black ink tattoos running together—animal faces, geometric shapes. You'll regret not having one, a permanent mark. You'll think, "Something to identify the body."

A woman will shriek out your name, and you'll dry yourself and follow her to the nail room, poorly ventilated and bright. You'll pick a sensible neutral. She'll ask how your day was. You'll smile and say, "Fine." You'll swallow a full sword.

You won't leave for five hours. Until it's dark. You'll fall asleep in a pink sauna lined with glowing bricks of a pink salt, small and silent with an aroma like bread. The ceiling will seem to pulse, and you'll close your eyes. You'll shower again and sit in the steam room, breathing in the thick, wet air. Filling your lungs with the heat. Exhaling through your mouth.

You'll schedule a scrub.

That's where you'll cry outright. The scrub will happen on a flat metal table. An older woman in black underwear will point to the slab without ceremony. You'll lay your body facedown, and she'll immediately douse you with scalding water. You'll wince, and she'll laugh. She'll coat your body in a rough soap and begin to sand off your legs, your stomach, your breasts, your arms. She'll flip you over like a hamburger patty and start again. When she rinses you off, gentler than before, you'll feel your skin wash down the table, your unnecessary cells. She'll touch your face, and you'll lean into her very slightly. You'll cry again. She'll say, "Too rough?" And you'll tell her, "It's fine."

When you come home, Charlie will greet you at the door. He'll be so worried—your phone was off. You'll fall headfirst into his chest and he'll catch you. You won't say a word, and when you look up at him, he'll be crying, too.

part two

YOUR MOTHER

PINK MILK

YOUR MOTHER AND I barely had a conversation from the time she was a very young child to when she announced she intended to leave the house at sixteen years old. We had very little in common and neither of us had much of an interest in forcing anything. I read on the couch and she read in her room, and she ate in the sunroom with the housekeeper at six while her brothers were at sports and I smoked in the kitchen waiting for your grandfather to come home. It was fine that way. It was quiet. Ships passing.

You have to consider, Bessie. I had three children by the time I was thirty-two. I had gone from this scrappy Brooklyn girl in this madcap love affair with your grandfather to being locked away alone in a big house in the suburbs while these three kids ran around and howled like hyenas. My world became very small very quickly. My sons could take care of themselves, but your mother was different. She needed me desperately. And she resented me when she sensed my distance. I'd look at her with her big brown eyes and she was this living, breathing reminder that there was something I could not give. I didn't have the perfect motherly instinct, because I was mourning the loss of a life I never had a chance to live. I'm not excusing myself. And I'm not saying I'm sorry. I'm just saying how it was.

It all went to hell the night before your mother started kindergarten. I'll never forget. I walked into her room—she must have been reading in bed with the housekeeper—and I set out her clothes on her rocking chair while they watched. I took out her patent leather Mary Janes from her closet, a powder-blue dress with mother-of-pearl buttons, a white cotton turtleneck, and little white bobby socks with ruffles at the cuffs. Perfect. She glared at me the whole time.

"Robbie, sit up so I can brush your hair."

She didn't know she had a choice then—those were the days. So she sat up on the edge of the bed and the housekeeper ran off, and I retrieved the Mason Pearson hairbrush from her dresser and got to work.

Her hair was thick and black and curly, and the only way to tame it was to brush it a hundred times. An enormous amount of hair on such a tiny girl. So I got to work and she moaned and she pretended to cry, and I held her shoulder and she wriggled away.

"Enough theatrics. If you tangle it, I'll have to start all over."

The first time she said "I hate you" was when I was brushing her hair. "I hate you." She couldn't have been older than seven.

She became very attached to the housekeepers as the years went on. There was a woman from Ireland who scrubbed a copper serving platter and it oxidized. An enormous Swedish woman who had a brain aneurism at the grocery store and died in front of half the town. A woman from the Caribbean who backed the car into a telephone pole and got out and ran down the street. An excommunicated nun who I think was an illiterate, but she made the most wonderful soufflé. Your mother charmed them all—and she turned them against me. She'd mock me with a singsong *"Yes, Mrs. Barbara"* if I asked her to do anything. None of the housekeepers lasted longer than a year.

They would look after her when your grandfather and I would leave for Europe for a month or two. I'd worry about your mother, building her case against me. Rifling through my purses for dollar bills and change. Throwing my cigarettes at the geese in the backyard.

I'd bring her back dolls from every country. A Spanish dancer holding miniature brass castanets. A Marie Antoinette from France with a porcelain face and rouge circles drawn on. A Hungarian soldier with a real mink hat. A couple of Dutch milkmaids in hand-painted clogs. She had a collection of fifteen or twenty by the time she was twelve, and she lined them up on the bookshelf across from her bed, staring at them as she fell asleep at night.

There was a woman we hired whom she loved in particular, Mrs. Garnier. Mrs. Garnier was from Montreal and her son was killed in a bar fight. She doted on your mother. She taught her to bake tarte tatin. When your mother practiced piano, Mrs. Garnier made up songs and sang along. One day while your mother was at school, Mrs. Garnier and I had a terrible fight—I forget about what—and she quit. She walked out of the house. That night your mother got her first headache.

They were not just headaches, they were crippling headaches—she'd wake up shrieking. She had ringing in her ears and pain she said felt like an electric jolt. Her vision would blur and she'd have to sit in the dark, rocking back and forth, until the headache stopped. They happened once a week, then twice. She came to me ranting and raving: "I can't go on like this. I'm dying." She collapsed on the floor. So I put her in the car and took her to Columbia-Presbyterian Medical Center.

She was seen by the top neurologist in New York. He did a full exam: vision tests, a scan of her head, something with electric pads. Nothing was the matter. Your mother wept in the car the whole ride back. "You can't make me live like this."

So I took her to the pediatrician in town, a lovely woman who'd seen all my kids since they were in diapers. She read through the report from Columbia and did some tests of her own. She said there wasn't anything to do. So I begged her. Robin needed help. I looked the doctor right in the eye and said, "You need to give her something." The doctor thought about it and suggested that perhaps your mother was suffering from some sort of seizure problem. It made sense to me. And so she wrote her a prescription for phenobarbital. It was only later I learned it's a version of the same drug they use to execute criminals.

Your mother was ten years old.

She started her regimen the next morning. It was a bright red syrup—cherry flavored—and I'd mix one big teaspoon in a glass of milk and she'd drink it with her breakfast. Pink milk. She did that for three years.

They were the greatest three years of anyone's life. She was calm and made all kinds of friends and did beautifully in school—she rose to the top of her class. At the end of each year they'd give out superlatives, and your mother was always awarded "smartest." She'd shake the principal's hand up there and everyone would cheer and she'd beam into the lights. We didn't get along any better, but we didn't fight, and that was enough. And everything was fine.

When she was eleven I sent her off to sleepaway camp with two bottles. In those days there was hardly any supervision. She started getting the doses wrong. She used a soupspoon to measure. So she'd make the milk too strong on some days and her tongue would turn red.

That's when she started to sleepwalk. She'd wake up in the middle of the night in the shower cabin, and on some mornings she'd have leaves in her hair. She'd apparently tried to break into the mess hall and fell asleep at the front door, which wasn't even locked.

One morning, when they played the bugle and all the girls woke up and made their beds and stood for inspection, your mother wasn't there. They searched the whole camp. They called a sheriff from the town in New Hampshire. They couldn't find her. They started searching the lake.

That afternoon, a man in a pickup truck was driving down the dirt road about three miles from the camp, and he saw what he thought was a garbage bag in a ditch. Your mother was sitting there in her nightgown, soaking wet in mud, shivering. When he dropped her off at the town hospital, the doctor asked if she'd been taking any medication, and she glared at him and said, "Ask my mother."

Oh, how I berated her when I got the call. I was worried, of course, but I knew she was fine. The doctor sent her back to camp with a measuring spoon.

Just after her thirteenth birthday, I drove your mother to the pediatrician to get the prescription refilled. Her bat mitzvah was the week before and it was perfect, if you must know—we had a luncheon at the house and she agreed to have her hair set and she wore a pale yellow skirt suit and cream pumps with one-inch heels. A miracle. (But, Bessie, *you* should never wear yellow with your coloring—you'll look dead.)

So I got to the pediatrician's office and the door was locked. I had somewhere to be, so I banged and I yelled, and your mother was rolling her eyes and giving me grief for getting the day wrong. Eventually we could hear someone starting to unlock the door from the inside. It took a full minute.

And standing there was the pediatrician, stark naked except

for a pair of glasses on a chain around her neck, her breasts pointed right at us. Her eyes were wild and her hair was sticking out at all angles. I shut the door. Your mother and I didn't say a word, and we got back in the station wagon. I drove her to school, and that was the end of the phenobarbital.

Years later, when your mother was at Columbia medical school, the doctor who initially examined her there passed away. He'd been the head of the neurology department for thirty-five years. There was a big ceremony and his picture was everywhere around the campus, and your mother recognized him. So she went to his office at his practice and she gave her name and requested her twenty-year-old records from his secretary, who was crying. She handed your mother a file folder: "Robin E. Bell, May 12, 1964."

And there was the diagnosis written in black ink: hyperosmia. Abnormally acute sense of smell.

PHONE CALL, DECEMBER 2011

GRANDMOTHER: Bessie?
GRANDDAUGHTER: *Grandma?*

Bess! Ha! Thank God in heaven I got you. You haven't left for Yosemite Park?
No, we're packing. We're about to get in the car. What's up?

You're going to be freezing! It's freezing there!
I know. I've packed a lot of warm layers and I'll be inside—

No, you won't. You'll be outside. Your mother says you're cross-country skiing.

Yes . . . Charlie's family really likes to cross-country ski.

I don't understand it. It's a ridiculous thing to do. It's not skiing, it's *shuffling.*

It's fun—it's being outdoors and it's not that hard. We practiced in Maine on a golf course.

But you're not going to be on a golf course. One fall and you snap your leg and you're lying there in the middle of the wilderness and you can't get up.

Surrounded by Charlie's family!

And how's that going to look? They take you outside for one second and you're belly up in a ditch.

Charlie led outdoor adventure trips for kids at a camp for five summers. I couldn't be with anyone more prepared for disaster.

You're not some ten-year-old boy he can throw in his backpack at a moment's notice. You're not exactly small.

[ASIDE]

Charlie, will you tell my grandma I'm not going to die in Yosemite.

CHARLIE: I'm not getting involved in this.

*Charlie says everything's going to be fine and he's very
prepared. I thought you were worried about me being cold.*

Can't I be worried about more than one thing? Why don't
they take you someplace normal? Even normal skiing—
somewhere with a hotel you can sit in.
    They like roughing it, being in nature.

Because they didn't come from suffering. They never chased
mice around the attic with a broomstick and survived on
forty dollars a week.
    I thought it was forty-five a week.

It was just enough to starve.
    Please just—

You know what's roughing it? Lying on a straw bed with
meningitis, and the only medication we can afford is cod liver
oil from the Italian neighbor whose son got his hand caught
in a meat grinder.

[SILENCE]

    Grandma, I think it's going to be fine.

Does your jacket have a lining?
    My jacket has a lining.

Bring a hat.

VOICE MAIL, ONE DAY LATER

Bessie, your grandfather says there are brown bears in Yosemite, and they've become domesticated because tourists are giving them food. But if they come up to you and you don't have any food, guess who they're going to eat? But they're not the worst of your problems. Grizzly bears are the real threat. If you even see a grizzly bear, it's already too late. I'm being serious, Bessie. You must be careful.

PHONE CALL, TWO DAYS LATER

GRANDDAUGHTER: *Grandma, I got your voice mail. I barely have reception—I'm standing in a field.*

GRANDMOTHER: Bessie, thank God.
I talked to Charlie and all the bears are hibernating.

That's a myth. They wake up and they eat.
The chances of me being attacked by a bear are extremely small. Speaking of animals, tomorrow we're riding horses! Horses are vegetarians.

Oh, Bessie. Oh my.
What did I say?

Have I told you about your mother's friend Lisa Belski?
Yes. The woman who didn't wear a helmet—

She was on her honeymoon in the South of France. And she and her new husband thought it would be a good idea to take a romantic ride on horseback through some vineyard or other. And they were riding along and your mother's friend Lisa's horse got spooked—who knows why? Maybe there was a bee! And the horse tossed her off and she landed on her head and she was *paralyzed* immediately. And then do you know what happened?

What happened?

Her husband abandoned her for a stewardess.

LEAVING IT ALL BEHIND

When your grandfather made his first money, we left Brooklyn for good. We had been living in the attic and then with Leo and Lily, and I had two children, your uncle Larry and your mother, who was just a baby. She had colic and the whole house would be up at night.

Your grandfather wanted to get as far from Brooklyn as possible, but I insisted we be along the train line to New York City, so we bought the house in Ardsley. It was a long and winding ranch house done in a contemporary style for the time, and I filled every inch of it with art. The dining room was enormous, and I had my mother's table extended with leaves and hung a chintzy bamboo chandelier with monkeys resting on the arms. It was very fashionable then. I thought it was fun. Bessie, when you come into an enormous amount of money very quickly, you have to do everything you can to make it seem like you've had it for ten generations.

I had the couches upholstered in a thick floral damask just like I'd seen in a photograph of a drawing room of a manor in the English countryside. There were real geodes from Brazil and masks from Africa that scared the living daylights out of your mother. I filled the walls with paintings from the Ashcan school, brooding men in hats crouched together in the cold; they reminded me of my father. They weren't pretty, but they were very fine works. I had a collector's eye.

I went to Christie's and I wasn't going to spend more than $1,000. I came back with a charcoal sketch by Milton Avery and a yellow print by a young artist from the Hamptons, Jackson Pollock. I spent $600 altogether. My hand to God. When the value went up—you'd kill me if you knew by how much—I didn't dream of selling it. I just bought a better frame.

There was a den off the dining room and I filled the built-in shelves with my books. In those days, women would buy these fake "decorator" books with cloth bindings to make it look like someone in their family might be a reader. I had all the classics from my brothers, of course—the Brontës and Austen and Mary Shelley and all her friends. I had the turn-of-the-century writers, Hemingway and Fitzgerald and Graham Greene. I had Mailer and Bellow and Updike and all the men who thought they knew better than anyone else about Jewish suffering. Ha. I had all my biographies—Stalin and Truman and Picasso—and all the writings on art and music and all the poetry I could fit. I'd read *The New York Times Book Review* for new books and those would join the pack. As the years went on, I fell in love with Coelho and Coetzee and all the prizewinners. Reading was very important to my brothers and it was important for me. I'd read a book and I'd imagine Leo grilling me about it: "Well, why did you enjoy it? It's not enough to enjoy it—it has to come to life and pinch you on the arm." The ladies at the club would marvel—"Bobby! Another book?"—as if I'd tucked my leg behind my head.

In 1965 your grandfather was working very hard at the factories and construction sites and trying not to get shot in an alley by the Mafia—he worked constantly in those years. The children were out of school, and I couldn't take it and I said, "Hank, you're taking a month off and we're going someplace quiet for the summer."

There was a man at the neighborhood pool named Lenny Demashkin, and he always went on and on about "the Vineyard" and how there were Jews there. So we packed the car and went to Martha's Vineyard. We rented a cottage in Chilmark for the summer, and we rented the same one the summer after that, and then years later your grandfather got his professorship at Columbia and we had full summers off, and so I said, "Hank, we're buying a house on the Vineyard right on the ocean."

In those days, there were the Jewish academics and there were the WASPs. Two separate enclaves. We found a real estate broker who sold "Jewish houses"—that's what they were called, because they'd been owned by Jews who had enough money and slipped through the cracks—and we bought the house on Stonewall Road. That's where we met our people.

They were different from our Ardsley neighbors; they were all academics from Harvard and MIT, and your grandfather was accepted into the gang because even though he was a philistine, he had stumbled his way into the Ivy League.

There was John, whom we met the summer before he'd win the Nobel Prize in Economics, and his wife and I got along. He's a dear man, and you'd never know he was the smartest person in the state at a given time. John and your grandfather shared a lobster pot in Menemsha Pond—blue and yellow stripes. The same colors as the Kennedys'! John and his wife would be at every Thanksgiving. They came to all the kids' weddings—John was at yours.

You saw John at the funeral, crying in the back row. He'd been widowed, too. Oh, his heart was broken for your grandfather. When he squeezed your hand and said, "I'm sorry, little girl," you knew he knew how much I loved you.

Ninety-one years old and he helped your grandfather carry my coffin from the building to the gravesite. That's John. Till the end.

The whole gang on the Vineyard was very smart. There was Alan. All of his daughters went to Radcliffe and went on to run various hospitals. There was Lev—he was Czech born—and one summer he was sure he'd win a big prize in mathematics, I think it was the Fields Medal, and one afternoon he got a call and was told he wasn't going to win after all. He returned to the beach after lunch, announced the news, walked around the bend behind the bluffs, and took off all his clothes and ran into the water naked. Nobody said a word.

We had our little enclave, but the rest of the island wasn't particularly welcoming toward Jews at the time. We had our place and the WASPs had theirs and the African American community had Oak Bluffs, where your grandfather and I would drive for a night out at a restaurant. At the Chilmark Community Center, there were square dances on the weekends, and the Christians would dance with the Christians and the Jews with the Jews, and the only time it was intermixed was softball. Your grandfather sprained both his wrists sliding into some red-faced stockbroker at home plate.

All afternoon we would sit on the beach, and the women were all "Harvard wives" and some of them had PhDs. But they accepted me immediately. Do you want to know why? I'll tell you. Books. They saw what I was reading on the beach: Tom Stoppard and Flannery O'Connor and William Styron, a book a week. So we talked books. We all had our big opinions. We argued and we shouted and it was wonderful. And so I made my friends there, and all winter in Ardsley I'd think about them.

Your mother was like me, a reader. You were, too, although God knows I never wanted you to be a writer. But I knew you would. I told you, Bessie—you should be a teacher. Make a salary. Have the summers off to travel. But you wouldn't listen. You never did. Neither did I. That's what made us friends.

EMAIL, 2010

SUBJECT museums

Bobby Bell bobby326@gmail.com   9/18/10
to me

visited the museum of art and design at columbus circle-it is sometimes called the popsicle museum . the quality of the crafts was great. i have always loved crafts. i saw the matisse exhibit also. it was fair.   am reading a good book called brooklyn by coim toibin. it is about an irish young woman coming to america. this is one of my first emails.love,grandma bobby

PHONE CALL, 2011

GRANDMOTHER: I'm very worried about your friend Emily.
   GRANDDAUGHTER: *Why are you worried about Emily?*

Because of the boy she's going with. The one who works at the not-for-profit in Brooklyn.
   You remember that?

Of course I remember that—I'm not an idiot!
   This I know.

She must break up with him.

And why is that?

Because if he's not going to move to San Francisco for her, forget it.
He has a job!

That's not a job. And besides, you're always out at night consoling her, and it's not good for your relationship with Charlie.
Charlie doesn't mind.

He does mind. Anyone would mind. You must pay attention to him.
I pay plenty of attention to my boyfriend.

And he'll *stay* your boyfriend!
What do you mean?

Nothing.
Grandma!

Forget I said anything. What do I know?
Charlie and I live together, we do everything together, he's very supportive, and I love him.

Then why doesn't he propose to you?
Because it's only been two years!

What does that matter?
Because it just does!

Bessie, you must cook for him at least five nights a week.

I cook all the time.

Two nights a week. It can't hurt.

Fine, fine. You're right.

I'm always right.

PHONE CALL, SEPTEMBER 2014

GRANDMOTHER: Bessie, did you land?

GRANDDAUGHTER: *Hi, hi—yes, I landed. I'm at the airport.*

Good. Order a car service.

I'm taking a cab. It's the same thing—it's actually much faster and less of a hassle.

Bessie, you must take a car service.

Nobody takes a car service!

That's not true. Everyone takes a car service—I see them all the time. Use the account. Call Skyline.

Fine. I'll call Skyline.

You're lying.

Of course I'm lying!

Bessie, I'm going to kill you.

    I don't care. Grandma, you don't have to worry. The only reason I'm not taking a subway is my ankle is in a—

Your ankle is in a what?

    Nothing. My ankle isn't in anything. It's fine.

You're lying to me.

    Grandma, I can take a cab from LaGuardia Airport to the Upper West Side.

Bess, do you know how much I worry about you?

    Enough to kill me!

Enough to kill you.

THREE CONVERSATIONS

STONEWALL BEACH, MARTHA'S VINEYARD, MEMORIAL DAY 2012

[PUTS DOWN HER BOOK]

GRANDMOTHER: Bessie, can I ask you a personal question?

    GRANDDAUGHTER: *Oh god.*

Bess Bell Kalb.

[PUTS DOWN HER BOOK]

Ask away.

What on earth are you doing with your life?
Excuse me?

You heard me.
Well. Presently, I'm trying to have a relaxing moment on the beach. But I guess that's shot to hell.

What are you doing at *Wires* magazine?
Wired. Wired magazine. It's a good magazine. It's owned by Condé Nast!

I don't care if it's owned by the Queen of Sheba. They're not letting you write.
They're paying me to fact-check.

You sit there scrubbing up another person's words while they get all the glory and you go home to Charlie and you're not you.
I'm pretty sure I'm me.

Is this what you want? Is this really and truly what you want?
Honestly, everyone starts somewhere and I'm paying my dues, and it's a good job in a bad economy, and Charlie's job is in San Francisco and Wired is the only San Francisco magazine that would pay me a living wage—

If you need money, I'll give you money.
I know. Thank you.

You're impossible.
  And besides, I love San Francisco.

Did you hear yourself?
  What?

How your voice went up?
  My voice stayed completely flat.

"I *love* San Francisco." Bull.
  Not bull! You saw it—you had a great time!

You put on a good show when I visited, but I know my granddaughter. San Francisco is for people who wear polar fleece to restaurants and try to convince each other to go camping.
  I like camping.

And I like getting shot in the head. What about that woman Nell?
  What about Nell? I haven't heard from her in a year.

But you went to Los Angeles and stayed with her and went on and on about all the writers for that cartoon you met.
  It's not a cartoon. It's The Simpsons.

Excuse *me. The Simpsons.* Why don't you write for *The Simpsons*?
  Ha! That's like me saying, "Why don't you lay a golden egg?"

Bessie.
 What?

If I wanted to lay a golden egg as much as you want to write
for *The Simpsons*, I'd lay a golden egg.
 So what would you have me do?

Call up Nell. Tell her you want to move to Los Angeles and
write for television.
 It's not that easy.

Can I ask you another question?
 Fine.

What would a man do?
 He'd call Nell and tell her he wants to write for television.

JUNE 2012

GRANDDAUGHTER: *Grandma, did you read the* Grantland
article?

GRANDMOTHER: I did. I have it right here. I've shown
everyone at the club.
 It's like ten pages long.

I sit there while they read it.
 Your poor friends.

They know what they signed up for. They're all proud of you.
Miriam. Sue-Ellen.
   Did you like it?

Like it? It was brilliant. Absolutely brilliant.
   Which part did you like best?

The part where it said "Bess Kalb" on the byline.

JULY 2012

GRANDDAUGHTER: *Grandma?*

GRANDMOTHER: Bessie, you sound like you're crying. Oh my
god—
   No, it's good. I got it. I got the job. The Jimmy Kimmel job.

Hank! She got it! Your grandfather is beside himself. He's
applauding from the other room. Oh, Bessie.
   Isn't that incredible?

No. Incredible would be if you didn't get it. It's entirely a
hundred percent appropriate.
   *I'm still crying. I have no idea what I'm doing, and they're
   giving me a thirteen-week trial period and then they'll
   probably fire me, and I have to move to L.A. and rent an
   apartment somewhere and I don't know what I'm going to
   do or what it is.*

Bessie.
What?

Get a blowout before your first day so your hair isn't a mess.
The rest you can handle.

LEAVING YOUR MOTHER

We'd come back from the Vineyard in the fall and I'd get very
tired and very blue. I hated the routine of it. How your mother
was constantly pushing me away, and I missed my friends
from school—Estelle in particular. I'd sit on a kitchen chair by
the phone and call her during the day. She was home now, too,
with her miserable husband.

I was hard on your mother. If she had a bad grade on an
exam, I'd yell and she'd cry. You'd think I hit her. I was trying
to motivate her. I couldn't stand to watch her become a burn-
out, to see her brilliance and her wit and her intellect and her
sheer force of will go to waste in some parking lot with hippie kids smoking marijuana and making plans to move to San
Francisco. I'd tell her, "Robin, if you don't succeed in school,
you'll never make your own money." And she'd fire back with
something real smart like, "It worked out just fine for you."

I didn't have a choice. She did. The world was changing
around her and I was terrified she was going to be swallowed
up by it.

But she couldn't see anything beyond my anger. She'd ask,
"Why do you hate me?" And I'd just stare at her across the
breakfast table, that long black hair of hers wild around her

Recuerdo Palacio Real Madrid

SOUVENIR · SANTORINI ·

GREECE

CATHEDRAL

OLD CANDEA

THE PORT

face, and I'd get up and say, "Robin, I don't hate you. I'd die for you." And she'd look at me and grunt. An incredulous grunt. She reminded me of my mother: serious. Strong-headed. My mother died just before she was born and I named your mother after her. "Robin," for Rose. You both got Rose's name in one way or another.

Nobody cried harder at my funeral. Not even your grandfather.

Your grandfather noticed how I'd changed in Ardsley and how I'd go to bed earlier and wake up later, and one day he looked at me as I was putting on my face in my bathroom. *My* bathroom. You want to know the secret to a long marriage? Separate bathrooms. So your grandfather said, "Bob, tell me what you need and I'll do it." He really meant it.

I told him, "I need to get away. Just the two of us." There was nothing your grandfather wouldn't do for me. So that's what we did.

We left for four to six weeks at a time. We went to all the great cities: Paris and London and Lake Maggiore in Italy, where Hemingway wrote *A Farewell to Arms*. Your grandfather would see me happy and it would make him elated. He'd say, "Can you believe our luck?" And I'd say, "Not in a million years." He'd hold me in his arms and we'd dance on verandas all drunk on local port, and for those moments everything would make sense.

We would stay at the grandest hotels—an ice cream sundae at two in the morning served in a silver bowl. Breakfast solariums overlooking the Swiss Alps, the hills of Provence, and the Aegean Sea. I don't know if it was the opulence or the distance from home, but whatever it was, it worked. This was before they had a name for the *malaise* and the torpor and whatever it was that takes hold of a woman trapped by her own circumstance. There wasn't lithium. There was the Ritz.

My mother fled through Europe, and half a century later I danced through it, Kir Royale in hand. How do you like that?

As the years went on and your mother grew into an adolescent, we'd leave for one of these trips and she would invite her friends over and throw parties. She'd open the liquor cabinet, let all the kids take what they wanted. Peter Luskin from down the street got so drunk he walked right through the plate glass sliding door to the backyard. It's a miracle he survived. I think he and your mother were going together at the time.

I'd come back and she'd be just awful.

When your grandfather and I returned from London one spring, I brought your mother back a beautiful season of clothes from a store on Carnaby Street. My favorite was a gorgeous lime-green shift with a white Peter Pan collar and matching coat and pillbox hat. I hauled it back to Ardsley and she took it out of the garment bag and laughed. She was in the ninth grade—it was the year she led the petition at her high school to allow the girls to wear pants. She'll tell you she did it for equality, but I think she did it to get back at me for forcing her into dresses.

Sometimes she'd start screaming fights with me that lasted a week. I don't recall what on earth they were about. Usually my cigarettes. She'd dump the whole pack in the toilet, and we'd have to call a plumber. Once I caught her emptying a whole carton in the powder room—you know, the room with the chinoiserie wallpaper. She flushed the toilet and yelled, "You're killing yourself, Mom!" I burst out crying and I told her, "Isn't that what you want?" and she stared at me. She let it hang in the air. After an eternity, she said, "No."

She'd storm out of the house and stay out overnight with her friend Jane—or at least that was the story I got. She refused to cut her hair and it went all the way down her back. I didn't dream of mentioning it.

I would lie awake at night fuming about her. I'd hit your grandfather in the arm and say, "Hank, what am I going to do about Robbie?"

He was soft. He doted on her. Always checking in from hotel lobbies and regaling her with stories about various cities and odd foods he ate. "Rob, you'd hate it. They eat nothing but frogs and snails!"

But he knew she was killing me. He told me, "Bob, if you can't beat her, join her." So I tried. When she insisted on wearing pants to school, I said, "Fine." I took her to Bloomingdale's in White Plains and I showed her the racks of beautiful corduroys and bell-bottoms and women's trousers. She was absolutely miserable. She stroked the cashmere twinsets and said, casually as anything, "Oh, look. Prison uniforms." She wouldn't try a single thing on. She marched out the door and waited sitting on the hood of the car, fuming.

Apparently Bloomingdale's was part of the "bourgeoisie" enemy that she was so desperately fighting against. She thought she was the first person to read Karl Marx and consider herself a revolutionary. She wasn't subtle. She'd call my high-heeled shoes "foot bindings," and when I complained my feet hurt, she'd say, "Men design them because they want us to limp." I'd say, "Isn't it nice to be so right about everything?" and she'd say, "It's agony."

On the way home from Bloomingdale's that day, I pulled into the parking lot of the army-navy store on Central Avenue and handed her all the cash in my wallet. "You want to look like a hippie? Look like a hippie." She got back in the car with a garbage bag full of moth-ridden clothes that smelled to high heaven. Stiff dungarees and men's sweaters and a ridiculous tweed blazer. She was ecstatic. Her whole wardrobe that year cost twenty-five dollars. Fine.

You wonder why she went to college at sixteen? It wasn't because she was some kind of genius—it was because she was angry with me. When she announced at the dinner table that this would be her last year at home, I was overjoyed. I admit it.

I've told you a million times by now how she made the deal with the principal. How she studied like a maniac and got a perfect score on the SATs, and he had no choice but to recommend her. But there's more to that story, Bessie. A lot more.

She made her announcement at the breakfast table over a pile of eggs and toast: "I'm going to college in the fall." I looked at her and I said, "Robin, if you want to go to college, then you're going to the best college." She was floored. She just glared at me, but she didn't put up a fight. She was as ambitious for herself as I was for her. You get it from both of us.

So I made some calls and I loaded her into the station wagon, and we drove up to New England for an eight-day road trip. One college a day. I bought her two suits, one gray and one navy blue, and she'd alternate them every other day and I'd always air the other one out by hanging it up in the backseat. Not a bad trick. It kept her dignified. Promise me you'll never wear the same thing two days in a row, even if nobody will notice.

It was 1971 and many of the schools hadn't integrated the girls, so I brought her to Barnard, Bryn Mawr, Radcliffe—ha—Jackson, Wellesley, and, finally, Pembroke. She fell in love with Pembroke immediately—the tour guide had armpit hair so long you could braid it. There were blond boys playing guitar out on the quadrangle with no shirts on. Heaven.

And she went back to Ardsley and went straight to the principal's office.

She told him, "If I get a perfect score on my SATs, you'll write me a letter of recommendation to Pembroke." She didn't ask. She told him. He laughed her out of his office. When he called me at home, he was still laughing. But by the end of the semester he was mailing the letter.

A month after that your mother got a thick envelope in the mail. "Congratulations, Robin Bell. You're in the first class of women admitted to Brown University, the class of 1975." She'd applied to one school and gotten into another. When I asked if she was disappointed, she said, "I'm *euphoric,*" and walked out of the room.

When I drove her up to Providence that fall, we didn't speak the whole way. And when I dropped her off at the dorm, she slammed the door, got her duffel bag and her suitcase, and didn't look back. Her long black hair in a braid swinging behind her. I drove down the hill and wept in the parking lot of a gas station for an hour. When I got back to New York my eyes were bloodshot and my throat was hoarse.

Your grandfather's face went white when he saw me. "Bobby, you look like you've been to war."

"Oh, Hank. I have."

VOICE MAIL, OCTOBER 2012

Bessie, your mother says you're angry with Charlie for keeping his job in San Francisco. You're being ridiculous. You're not going to stay in Los Angeles forever. You burn in the sun and you're a terrible driver. And you really have no idea how long the Jimmy Kimmel job will last. They could fire you. Your mother says there are only two other women on the staff and you've never written for television before. What do you think you're going to do? Become a comedian?

Though it's true that when you were a little girl you used to do a comedy routine by the pool in Florida. It was very good. You must have been five years old. You'd walk up to the old people on their lounge chairs with their families and say hi. They all knew you: "Robin's daughter"—already you had the exact same face. So you'd say hi and they'd ask you how your year was going, and you'd smile very sweetly and say, "Funny you ask. I learned to say the alphabet backward." They'd be in shock. You were this little imp with these big blue eyes, very sincere. They always took the bait. "Really? Can you do it now?" You'd grow very serious, clear your throat, turn your back to them, and say the alphabet.

Anyway, don't be angry with Charlie. Wait it out. Mark my words: he'll move for you just like you moved to San Francisco for him. One of the things you got from me was your ability to hold a grudge. We don't tolerate being wronged. It isn't a good quality. It won't serve you. Let it go. That boy loves you. He loves you *even though* he knows who you are. He worships the ground you walk on and he's exactly right.

Rebook your ticket to Oakland for Friday.

THE MEXICO STORY

On Christmas Day 1968, your grandfather and I left for Mexico City. We intended to stay for three weeks.

Five days in I got a call from your mother. "Mom? I think I'm in trouble."

It was the year after the Chicago Seven rioted at the Democratic National Convention and got arrested. A group of seven boys so opposed to the Vietnam War they decided to start a countercultural revolution. Your mother was a sophomore in high school and she had become enamored with them. It's no coincidence your father looks like Tom Hayden. And all throughout that fall semester, she and two of the boys in her class had been organizing on their behalf. They had a cause. They had been trying to raise money for the legal fund. Can you believe it? Three teenagers from a Podunk town in Westchester thought they'd lead the brigade to free the most notorious political protesters of the year from jail. Of course I supported the cause—I was the one who protested the war in Washington—but I think there's a way to do it without winding up in jail. Your mother disagreed. What else is new?

You have to understand. Your grandfather worked to get us out of poverty. Five years before your mother was born, I was wearing your grandfather's dungarees to the grocery store in winter because I couldn't afford nylons and a long enough coat. Twenty years before, I was eating gristle a cousin had stolen off a truck in the Meatpacking District. A generation before that, my mother was on a boat clutching her sack full of tinned fish without two nickels to her name. And in 1968, we had finally made it, Bess. Assimilated almost completely. And here was your mother, ungrateful at every turn, threatening to throw it all away. It wasn't her politics I opposed. It was her hubris.

And it was hardly original. This was 1968, and kids were taking hallucinogenics and smoking marijuana and getting on buses to San Francisco and never coming back. In her mind, she was being some sort of revolutionary. Really, Bess, she was following the pack. Right over a cliff.

Back at the school, your mother and her friends made pamphlets. They had buckets to collect coins set up in the cafeteria. They gave speeches in study halls about the injustice and the "military-industrial complex"—her words—and they were pissing off whomever they could. Shouting in bullhorns in the teachers' parking lot. Imagine how my father would have loved her.

The high school board in Ardsley at the time was run by very conservative Methodists and Episcopalians from the town. Word had gotten around and they weren't thrilled with what your mother and her friends were doing. There was talk of expulsion. What your brilliant mother was doing violated every imaginable policy: she and her little gang were raising money for a political cause on school grounds.

By the end of the semester, she had contacted the lawyer representing the Chicago Seven. The actual lawyer. At the time he was with the ACLU. She wrote him a letter on behalf of herself and her friends explaining the situation—how they were sacrificing their education for the cause. They were so proud of themselves. The lawyer wrote them back immediately. He loved them, these high school kids. And he had an idea. Your mother and her gang would be a test case. He told them to keep doing what they were doing, to write a manifesto declaring their intent to keep beating the drum for the Chicago Seven's release in violation of school policy, and once expelled, he would help them sue the school board.

Can you imagine? *Bell v. Board of Education*. Robin Ellen Bell. A sacrificial lamb marching proudly toward the slaughter.

She drafted the manifesto in one night. I read it later. It was soaring—very pompous and completely inflammatory. She called the president of the board a "capitalist pig." All that from a child who lived in a big house on a full acre abutting a gated, neighborhood-only swimming pool. She wrote it up and was ready to mimeograph it and post it all throughout the hallways the next day.

That night, as I was putting on my earrings in our room at the Gran Hotel Ciudad, we got a call from the front desk. "Mrs. Bell, someone named Robin just called for you, but she hung up." She used her first name. Not "your daughter."

So I took the stairs down to the lobby in one earring and my bathrobe and my sneakers still muddy from our hike, and I shut myself into one of the phone booths in the lobby. The answering machine picked up. I had never been more infuriated to hear my own voice. I called again. And again. And on the third try, she answered.

"Mom?"

"What have you done?"

"What do you mean 'what did I do'? Nothing!"

"Robin. Spit it out."

She told me about the Chicago Seven—which was ridiculous; I'd given them money when they were the Chicago

Eight—and she told me about how she'd convinced those two poor kids to go along with her and how she wrote the manifesto and about the lawyer and everything.

My voice was very calm, but you should have seen me, clenching the phone in a half-open robe, gritting my teeth so hard they should've turned to dust.

But I sounded very even. If I hadn't, she wouldn't have listened. She wouldn't have stayed in school and aced her exams and gotten into Brown and had her first marriage and gone to Israel and gone to Paris and gone to medical school and met your father and had you.

"Well, Robin, it sounds as if you've made up your mind to sign it."

"I'm not sure if I should sign it."

"Oh, really?" I was practically singing.

"I don't know?"

"Why wouldn't you sign it? You feel so passionately—"

"You're being condescending. I'm hanging up."

"Go right ahead!"

There was silence. Then I heard her sigh so loudly I had to hold the receiver away from my ear. It was all very dramatic.

"I'm not signing it."

"How come?"

"Because I want to get into college and get the *fucking hell* away from you."

I wanted to hop in a taxi in my robe and fly back to New York and wring her neck. But I did something much worse.

I said, "Good. Go."

She didn't sign the thing. And she went.

PHONE CALL, DECEMBER 31, 2012

GRANDMOTHER: Happy New Year, Bessie!
GRANDDAUGHTER: *Happy New Year, Grandma!*

What are you and Charlie up to?
We're in Mexico. We'll just have dinner at the hotel and probably just go to bed early.

Is it a nice hotel?
It's beautiful, but it's very rustic. It's a yoga retreat and there are open-air little huts right on the ocean. Our friends are working there for the season and so we got a discount.

I don't even know where to begin.
What do you mean?

You'll be eaten alive by mosquitoes sleeping in the open air.
There's mosquito netting! Anyway, what are you and Grandpa—

You're sleeping in a net and anyone can just walk in off the beach and take what they want.
It's in a very remote area.

Perfect. No police. Not that it matters. It's all cartels there now.
You're scaring me.

Good.

Anyway, I'm doing a lot of yoga. First thing in the morning and every evening at sunset. I've never done more exercise in a single week.

[PAUSE]

That's excellent.
   Yes, it is.

Bessie.
   What?

Go stay at a normal hotel. Stay at a resort. Use my card.
   Grandma, we're staying here. I don't want to stay at a resort. That's not our vibe.

"Not our vibe." I have no idea what you're talking about. When they come at you with machetes, don't say I didn't warn you.
   I'm more terrified of you than the cartels.

That's the first smart thing you've said all day.

THE ANNULMENT

I know you know that your mother was married once before your father. She was a kid, barely twenty-two. Two years out of college. She was tough. She wouldn't listen. She didn't care what I thought about anything until she had you.

She met this man just after she got back from living on the kibbutz and almost dying in Paris. I've told you about how she decided to become a doctor in that hospital in Paris and I told her I'd help her. Your grandfather was furious. He wanted her to go into urban planning. But there was no sense in arguing, and so I drove her to Harvard to take night classes in chemistry and biology at the extension school. She hadn't taken chemistry since the tenth grade, and there was no way she'd get into any decent medical school if she didn't know the subject. But she was brilliant, fortunately, and in a few months she hardly needed to study to do well in the class.

That year, she kept coming across this very handsome young man all around campus. He'd be at the library when she was there. He'd be smoking Parliaments outside the biology department when she left class. He and your mother would go to the same falafel place, and she'd see him eating out of his pita pocket with a knife and fork.

His name was James. He was from the Upper East Side of Manhattan; his father was a big-time newspaper editor and his mother descended from someone on the *Mayflower*. A real WASP—square jaw, upturned nose. A blue blood. And he noticed your mother. She wasn't like the other girls in their twinsets and peacoats. She wore her hair in a long braid and she always had these terrible silver bracelets clanking around her wrist and clunky army boots. And he wasn't anything like the boys your mother went with at Brown. He'd never gone two weeks without a haircut in his entire life.

Do you want to know how he got your mother's phone number? He stopped her on the street and demanded it. Like a stickup. He didn't ask for it; he said, "Today is the day I get your phone number." Bessie, beware of men who have gone their whole lives without hearing the word "no."

He was studying to become a doctor in the same program and he was working as a lab assistant at a hospital at night. They rarely saw each other through the whole courtship, and they dated for four months and he decided they'd get married. He decided. He announced it to your mother: "Robin Bell, you're going to be my wife." They never lived together before that.

James got into Columbia medical school at the end of your mother's first year, and she dropped out of the program and the two of them moved into a cheap apartment in Riverdale with an air conditioner that leaked water all over the floor. Did you have any idea that when you went to high school up there she used to drive right by the building every morning, never saying a word?

They settled into their apartment and he was to be the doctor and she was to abandon all her premed studies and get a job and support him and be his wife. She wanted desperately to be a doctor, but she loved him madly. He was the great genius, the great man. She cut her hair and straightened it every day and started taking an aerobics class at the YMCA. She once mentioned to him she'd go back to school when he was established in his career and making a salary, and he laughed and didn't look up and said, "You'll have your hands full with the rug rats by then." He really said that. Rug rats. Imagine being as smart as your mother and not seeing a single warning sign?

So that summer I threw her the most perfect wedding money could buy. It was under a white tent in the backyard, and all the waiters were in matching red vests and red fezzes, like at one of the grand hotels in Morocco. I wore a stunning orange-and-pink Pucci dress, which at the time was very avant-garde. You can buy as many clothes as you like, Bessie, but you can't buy style. There was a champagne tower and a live jazz band, and everyone danced until there wasn't any alcohol left. Nobody ever said I couldn't throw a party.

The marriage went sour fast. Your mother would call me from the pay phone on the street and I'd hear cars honking and ask, "Why aren't you calling from the apartment?" And she never had a decent answer. One morning I drove by the apartment to drop off some wedding presents that had been sent to Ardsley, and she was wearing dark sunglasses and turned me away, which I thought was odd. She had specifically asked for the chairs! One night during one of her pay phone calls, I swear to God I heard her sniffling. In all her life she had never called me crying. I asked her what the matter was and she said, "Nothing." And then she said, "I don't know. I think I'm just difficult." And I closed my eyes and felt the ground drop beneath me.

I knew that tone of voice. I knew it from Estelle.

You know that story about your grandfather paying him off. But I don't think you have any idea what I did. Your grandfather isn't the only hero of this particular story. He was the muscle.

One afternoon your mother called me up from her apartment, cheery and bright as can be, and she told me, "I think I'd like to go see Marian, but James is taking the car this afternoon." Marian was her closest friend from Brown. She lived in Halifax. She had flown in for the wedding and stayed at our house. And I said, very nonchalantly, "Oh, for how long will you see Marian?" And she said, "Maybe until dinner." And I said, "Doesn't Marian live in Canada?" And your mother said, "Certainly. Yes. Yes, that's right." And the line went quiet. And her tone of voice was very odd when she repeated, "But I'll be back in time to have dinner with James."

Something was very off. So I said, "Stay exactly where you are."

I was in front of her at the curb in about forty-five minutes with a suitcase full of my underwear and socks and sweaters and a winter coat. I drove her straight to Kennedy Airport. She boarded a seven p.m. flight to Halifax and went off to stay with Marian. She didn't say thank you; she just walked to the ticket counter with my suitcase in her hand.

Then I dealt with James.

He never particularly cared for me, and he resented the checks I occasionally sent your mother. But I knew he was terrified of your grandfather. He respected him—he was a department chair at Columbia, after all. I went home, and that same night, I sent your grandfather right back to Riverdale with a blank check. It must have been two in the morning when he got there. He opened their apartment door—we had the key. He took that guy by the collar of his shirt and said, "How much for you to walk away?" James looked your grandfather straight in the eye and he said, "Twenty thousand dollars." Your grandfather took out his pen and the checkbook he carried in his jacket pocket and said, "I'll make it an even five." And that was that.

Everyone has a price.

PHONE CALL, NOVEMBER 2012

GRANDDAUGHTER: *Hi, Grandma.*

GRANDMOTHER: Bess! What's wrong? What's the matter? *Nothing's the matter! I'm just calling you back. I'm just getting out of work.*

It's seven at night your time! *The show tapes at six and I stayed to watch it. I had a bit on! With kids—it's cute. I'll send you the link.*

You're working yourself too hard. You and Charlie should enjoy being engaged.

I'm enjoying being engaged by living my life and doing my job.

You're like your mother. You sound very anxious. This whole thing is killing you. You know what you should do? You should become a teacher.
Grandma.

You like working with kids so much. And you can be a teacher anywhere. You can be a teacher in New York.
I can think of two reasons why I should not become a teacher: I need a master's degree and I have no interest in becoming a teacher.

I have three reasons why you should.
Try me.

June, July, and August.

PHONE CALL, JANUARY 2013

GRANDDAUGHTER: *Grandma. Great news. I found my wedding dress.*

GRANDMOTHER: I thought you already bought your wedding dress!
I'm selling the long one and I'm getting a short one—tea length.

[SILENCE]

Grandma?

I'm here.
  You're upset.

Why would I be upset? It's your wedding.
  I just didn't feel like myself in the one from New York. I felt like a cupcake.

All right.
  And it was really heavy. I wouldn't have been able to dance.

All right.
  My mom wore a tea-length dress.

It was her second wedding, Bessie.
  It was beautiful. I'd wear it, but I can't wear a drop waist because of—

Because you have my hips! Thank you, Grandma!
  Thank you, Grandma.

Just tell me it's white.
  It's white. It's all in a delicate lace with a fitted strapless bodice and tulle under the skirt. It feels like a ballerina's dress.

Fine.
  I really love it.

You'll need to wear a strapless bra.
  *It actually doesn't even need a bra because of the structure
  of the bodice.*

Wear a bra. You'll thank me.
  I always thank you.

That's right.
  Anyway, what are you going to wear?

I was thinking I'll wear yellow. I saw a yellow Armani jacket
in bouclé that will be perfect for June.
  It sounds very elegant.

Well, I'm very upset I can't wear the skirt. My legs have these
horrible veins!
  *So wear pants! It's cold in June anyway! You'll look great in
  pants.*

Fine.

[BEAT]

Bessie?
  Yes, Grandma?

You're going to look stunning.

VOICE MAIL, TWENTY MINUTES LATER

Bessie, oh, your cell phone is probably on silent. What am I going to do with you? Have I ever told you about my wedding dress? My brother Leo's wife, Lily, sewed it herself on a dress form. But it was very ornate—big sleeves and a high lace collar and a full ball-gown skirt. I wasn't sentimental about it. When your mother was a little girl, I'd give it to her and she'd play dress-up with it with her friends. They'd run around the backyard in it doing plays. It was torn to shreds. I never cared. What do I care? It was the same backyard where your mother got married. Twice.

The first time she wore an elaborate dress. She hated it. I insisted on it.

When your mother married your father, she was doing her medical internship, she was exhausted. Two times I met her for lunch and she had a patient's blood in her hair. So it was time to buy a dress and we went to Saks, and whatever they had is what she got. Off the rack. It was an afternoon dress. Not even formal.

The older you get, the more you remind me of her.

TWO VERSIONS OF THE SAME STORY

1

Your mother would kill me for saying this, but you weren't exactly "planned."

She had just passed her medical boards—it was the second

year of her medical residency—and she went out drinking. Gin and tonics all night. Enough to give her quinine poisoning. You'd think she was trying to cure malaria. A few days later she was still throwing up. She felt awful. She thought she was dying. So she went into the emergency room and the doctor took one look at her. "When was your last menstruation?" She thought for a minute, then she threw up on his shoes. There's your answer. And you wonder why you love gin.

So nine months later you still weren't born. She was in terrible pain. Every time I checked in on her it was one complaint after another: "My back is killing me—I can't walk. I can't sleep. I think they're wrong about the baby. I think it's twins." She was working up until the end, her belly stretching out her hospital scrubs—a reminder of what happens when you let a *woman* in the program (there were only two other women in the psychiatry rotation at Columbia). She'd joke about it when patients brought it up. "I had a big lunch."

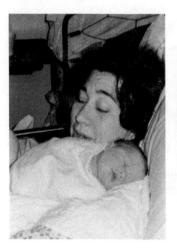

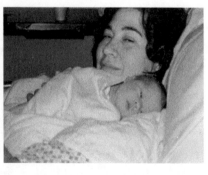

At forty-one weeks she refused to go in and get induced. She wouldn't even talk about a cesarean section. I'd tell her to get it over with and she'd hang up. You two were already playing chicken.

It was thirteen days past her due date and she was waiting for her omelet at Popover Café on Eighty-sixth and Amsterdam when her water broke all over the leather booth. She said "shit" loud enough that a busboy ran over. She left ten dollars cash on the table and marched out the door and hailed a cab and was at New York Hospital by eight a.m.

Someone paged your father, who was doing his critical care rotation at Mount Sinai, and he ran into the room at 8:20. It was just him and a nurse and your mother—their doctor was on his way from Westchester, but there wasn't any rush, they thought, because the labor had barely started. The nurses changed shifts at nine a.m.—everyone in the north tower and south tower walked across the skybridge and switched places. You shot out at 9:02 into a bewildered doctor's hands. He was paged to the next delivery, and he looked at your father and said, "You're a physician, right?" Your father nodded and the doctor handed you to him. Then he left and it was just your mother and your father and all of you blinking at each other in disbelief. The covering doctors heard a baby cry and ran in all hysterical. They cut the cord and checked all your functions (perfect), cleaned you off, and put you on your mother's chest.

You both got very quiet, and then you looked away from her and fell asleep.

When I came into the room an hour later, she said, "Mom, what am I supposed to do?"

2

Your mother was thirty-two when she decided it was time to have you.

She had just finished the first year of her medical residency and had decided to go into psychiatry. She had finally found what she loved: unlocking people's minds, reassembling their sanity, healing the anguish in their heads with her wits and instinct. She'd written her admissions essay about the pink milk I'd given her when she was a girl and how she wanted to fight that kind of misdiagnosis. Blame me.

She had also found something else she loved: your father. Your father was her champion. Nothing like James. He was four years younger than she was, but she was a year behind him in medical school because she'd taken so much time off to nearly die in Paris and accidentally marry a schmuck. Your father was the top student in his class—a brilliant scientist, an intuitive physician. A healer. When they met, he invited her up to his dorm room at Columbia medical school and said, "Would you like a panini?" She had no idea what he was talking about, but she said, "Sure." He took out fresh bread and aged cheddar and whole grain mustard from a dresser drawer, plugged in an electric contraption, and made your mother the greatest cheese sandwich she'd had in her life. The way he watched her eat it made her know he'd put her delight above anything else so long as he drew breath. She wasn't wrong. Four years later, they were married.

And two years after that, your father took her to St. Barth's to celebrate before she took her board exam. They stayed at a ramshackle bed-and-breakfast in the middle of the jungle.

It was owned by a young bohemian couple who had come to the island on vacation and never left. Can you imagine? There were goats and chickens and a garden where they grew all the vegetables they ate. They had two little twin boys with long blond hair running around the place barefoot and they all lived this very charmed life.

By the end of the trip, the boys had taught your mother how to break a coconut and climb a tamarind tree to pick the fruit. She was relaxed and tan and happy. On the last night, she leaned over to your father at the big communal dinner table and said, "Let's have a kid." He could have died of happiness right then and there.

As you grew inside her, she'd walk by the children's clothing stores on the Upper West Side and marvel at the dresses. Little blue-checked pinafores and lace booties. Hats printed with tiny ducks. Pink this, pink that—all this stuff she'd never buy for herself. She stockpiled it all.

At work, her patients would touch her belly when she examined them. "Is it a boy or a girl?" they'd ask, and she'd grin and say, "Girl," as if she'd won the lottery. She'd feel you kick at night and wake up, then sing you back to sleep: *"Youuu can dance, youuu can ji-ive, having the time of your li-ife . . ."*

You were two weeks late. It was freezing on January 29, but she insisted on going for a walk that morning anyway. She made it two blocks to Popover Café on Eighty-sixth and Amsterdam and was just sitting down in a booth when her water broke. She shouted, *"Thank God!"* loud enough that a busboy ran over. She threw ten dollars on the table and marched outside and hailed a cab.

"New York Hospital! I'm having a baby!"

When you were born, the nurses were changing shifts and it was just you and your mother and your father in the room. The three of you, all alone for a full minute. She looked from your father to you and she closed her eyes and sank into the pillow. "Bess. Her name is Bess."

YAHRZEIT

I've been dead a year.

It's getting harder for you to hear my voice in your head, and you won't listen to the voice mails you saved.

You collected them for years, which is both sentimental and morose.

Listen to them. I'll wait.

Greeting	**Voicemail**	Edit
Grandma Palm Beach mobile	1/27/17	0:17
Grandma Scarsdale mobile	10/23/16	0:11
Grandma Scarsdale mobile	10/23/16	0:27
Grandma Scarsdale mobile	10/16/16	0:24
Grandma Scarsdale mobile	10/2/16	0:16
Grandma Vineyard mobile	8/3/16	0:16
Grandma Scarsdale mobile	5/16/16	0:15
Grandma Palm Beach mobile	4/20/16	0:13
Grandma Palm Beach mobile	2/4/16	0:23

Greeting	**Voicemail**	Edit
Grandma Palm Beach mobile	2/2/16	0:26
Grandma Scarsdale mobile	11/2/15	0:32
Grandma Vineyard mobile	7/11/15	0:25
Grandma Palm Beach mobile	2/1/15	0:38
Grandma Palm Beach mobile	1/7/15	0:34
Grandma Scarsdale mobile	11/25/14	0:24
Grandma Scarsdale mobile	11/25/14	0:32
Grandma Scarsdale mobile	11/12/14	0:39
Grandma Scarsdale mobile	10/27/14	0:43

You won't do it. You're afraid you'll cry or that they'll be very banal. Here. I'll say them for you.

Hi, sweetheart. It's Grandma. Call me back.

Hi, honey. It's Grandma. I was wondering if you and Charlie had any plans for New Year's. We're going to the club down here. Anyway, call me back.

Bessie, it's Grandma. I just got the new J.Crew catalog in the mail and I am calling to tell you to buy a peacoat. You won't look good in the camel color. Buy it in black. Anyway, call me.

Bessie, you must call your mother. She's worried about you hosting all those people in Block Island. They're adults. They can take care of themselves. Your stomach can't handle all the stress.

Yeah, hi. Grandma. Call me back.

Bessie, your mailbox was full. Do you need a new dress for that girl's wedding in Thailand? You know it's very hot there. Call me back.

Bessie, I just saw the most mediocre film. It was the Steve Jobs biopic. Don't watch it. Very plodding and all over the place thematically. Your grandfather loved it.

Bessie, I can't tell you how upset I am. Frances died. Oh, Bessie. Oh my. She was only eighty-five. It was a stroke. Oh, Bessie. I'll try you back.

Bess. The New York Times *is saying they put formaldehyde in the hair-straightening treatment you do. You must stop. I'll mail you the article. Just get blowouts a couple times a week like everyone else on the planet.*

Bessie.

Bessie, it's me. Grandma. I'm just around.

Yeah—hello. Bessie, it's me. I'll give you another ring.

Bessie, hello.

Bessie, I'm just calling.

Bess.
It's me.
It's Grandma.

Just listen to them. Hear my voice. I'm right there, in your phone, in your bag. I'll wait. Listen to them. I'm slipping from you. Fading. It's terrible to fade. I could be very close. In your ear, clear as a bell, asking you to call me back.

{ part three }

OUR LIFE TOGETHER

I'VE NEVER TOLD YOU about the first time I held you in my arms.

It was the day you were born. You were two weeks late, so I was already camped out in a hotel room in New York.

You already know the story of the water breaking and the nurses changing shifts. How your grandfather and I were there within the hour.

I put on a yellow smock and a hairnet and walked into the delivery room. Your mother was asleep in her hospital bed and your father was tending to her, stroking her hair. I walked straight to you in your bassinet.

You had these little bow lips, round rosy cheeks. You were fair, like me, with milky gray eyes, like me, and reddish hair. Nothing like your mother right from the start. You opened your eyes, bleary and wet and narrow. I wiped some schmutz off your chin. I touched your forehead with the back of my hand. You made a squawk and I squawked back. I scooped you very carefully out of the bin, and I pressed you to my chest and breathed in your head. I'd never done anything like that before. And I held you about a foot away from my face and you had your little eyes open, fixed on my face. You didn't have a name yet, so I gave you one. "Hello, angel. Hello, my angel."

There you were, staring at me out of my own eyes. Perfect.
Just perfect.

PHONE CALL, FEBRUARY 2013

GRANDMOTHER: Hi, honey, how's everything going?
GRANDDAUGHTER: *Everything's fine.*

Just fine?
I'm just making dinner. It was a long day.

You work too hard. The job is too much for you. Your mother
says you fall asleep working with your laptop on your chest.
I'm fine. I can handle it.

Where's Charlie?
He's at his coworking space downtown.

And your mother said his remote job doesn't pay the rent on that office.
It's a human rights organization and their budget goes toward crisis response software—

It doesn't matter. They have plenty of funding. He should insist the company pays the rent for his office.
Maybe he should have you call them.

Very funny. What are you cooking anyway?
Salmon from a New York Times *recipe.*

Oh, I love to make salmon.
You make salmon?

Of course I make salmon. I just put it in the microwave on high.
And that works?

Sure.
I don't think I'm going to do that.

Bessie, can I say something?
What?

Throw out the fish and order some decent food. Nobody wants to come home to salmon.

NURSERY SCHOOL

Have I ever told you what happened on your first day of nursery school? It was two buildings down from your parents' apartment. Your mother had just gone back to work. Oh, how you'd cry when the babysitter tried to take you out of the house! And I was in Florida—your grandfather and I had bought the apartment in Palm Beach a few years before, and we were spending half the year there. So I got the call: "Mom? Can you take Bessie to school?" I hung up and got on a plane. She didn't even finish her next sentence.

We walked into the school, took the elevator up, and when the doors opened you squeezed my hand so hard it almost fell off. You looked straight ahead like I was marching you off the plank. I crouched down to hug you goodbye. You started breathing fast, and your little heart was beating right through your coat and tears started streaming down your cheeks at full force. Big, round tears. I thought someone would call the police. So I took your red face in my hands and looked you in the eye, and I said, "Angel, I'll be right here. Right outside this door. I'm not going anywhere." You stopped crying. You knew I wouldn't lie to you. You didn't even ask me to promise, you just wiped your eyes with your two hands and walked right in.

Thank God I had *The New York Times* in my handbag.

Two minutes later—maybe one minute—I heard a little knock on the door. That was our code. So I popped my head up so you could see me through the window on the door and gave you a big, wide smile. "Everything's okay! You're all right! Grandma's here." You nodded and headed back to the circle of kids. Then five minutes later—*knock-knock-knock-knock-*

knock!—and I popped up through the window and smiled. Then ten minutes, twenty, thirty, and so on. But all day, unless you were napping, you'd give a knock and there I'd be, smiling like a showgirl, letting you know it would be all right. I'm here. You're safe.

I didn't get through a single article.

It happened all week. By Friday, you didn't knock. That's when I cried.

MY PET

You said your first words to me and you also stood up for the first time when I was there.

I would fly to New York every week when your mother was finishing her residency, and I'd sit with you in the apartment and hold you in my arms and talk to you until you said something back. Waiting for you to mirror my words.

When you were seven or eight months old, I was pacing around on the cordless phone in the living room in the house on Martha's Vineyard, ranting and raving and waving my free arm around in the air. You yelped out for me so I'd pay attention, then pulled yourself up by the edge of the low wooden coffee table and gave me a big wave and a smile. I stopped in my tracks. I turned off the phone and I waved back. "Oh, hi, angel!" You let go of the table and teetered around for a second or two and fell smack down on your tush, as astonished as I was. Thank God you didn't fall forward.

Two years later you would put on my red high-heeled pumps and parade around the house yelling, "Hank! Robin!

Bessie!" A riot. You would open my jewelry drawers and carefully examine each piece in its individual felt square. You'd pick up the rings and marvel at them sparkling in the light. You'd try on the enamel bangles and shake them around, and you'd run the strands of pearls between your fingers. All of them your treasures. I'd always say the same thing: "You want it? One day it'll be yours." "What day?" "When you're a little older." And I'd give you a junky pin or an amber beaded necklace, and you'd be ecstatic and we'd leave it at that.

You'd sit on one of the cushioned stools in my powder room and watch me apply my lipstick. My mouth stretched open in a wide circle as I coated my lips in a bright shade of coral. Then I'd whip out a tissue from its silver box, fold it in half, rest it in my mouth, and smack my lips together on it. You must always blot or it'll clump up and settle around the edges and you'll look like an old fortune teller.

You begged your mother for a lipstick when you were in the third grade. I got a call from your mother.

"She said you let her wear your *makeup*."

"Oh, please. We have fun."

"Mom. She's a kid. She plays kickball."

"All little girls want to wear lipstick."

"I didn't."

"No kidding."

Click.

When you were twelve years old, you came down to Palm Beach for winter break all by yourself for the first time. I waited for you at the gate, and as you stepped into the terminal we charged for each other like bulls.

Every morning we brought our books to the pool and sat out under big hats with zinc on our noses. We ate cantaloupe slices at the kitchen table and talked about whatever there was to say. We went to Neiman's and Saks, and I bought you a lavender linen scarf you wore every single day for a year.

One afternoon I took you along to my beauty parlor appointment on Worth Avenue, and I asked the girl to blow-dry your hair straight. You sat in the chair reading your book, and I looked at you and I couldn't believe how lucky I was.

My pet.

Your mother never let me hear the end of it.

It was almost as bad as the time I cut off a lock of your hair when you were a very little girl. She made a federal case out of it. You'd think I shot you in the head. You had the most beautiful hair when you were three or four—a very light reddish brown with streaks of gold through it. We were alone in the apartment after nursery school, and I took a pair of kitchen shears and chopped off a curl. You didn't mind. Besides, I asked you!

"Can Grandma have a piece of your hair?"

I'll never forget what you said.

"Can I have it back?"

I laughed. "Sure!"

I cut it off, put it in a Ziploc, and it stayed in my handbag for a year. I took it to every appointment at every beauty salon. "Match this."

WEDDING DAY, JUNE 2013

[IMMEDIATELY AFTER THE LAST SPEECH]

GRANDMOTHER: Bessie.

GRANDDAUGHTER: *What's wrong?*

Nothing! Absolutely nothing.

Why have you been pacing around for the past twenty minutes?

You shouldn't have sat the rabbi next to Charlie's father.

Why not?

Because this rabbi you found happens to be the most boring man on earth.

Excuse me?

You heard the ceremony.

Yes. I was there.

All he did was talk about the Torah and the Talmud and recite *Hebrew*.

That's his job. Grandma, that's literally his one job. And we had like two prayers maximum. Per your request.

The rabbi is boring Charlie's father.

No, he's not. Look at them! He's laughing.

He's not laughing. He's just being polite. He has good manners because they all went to boarding school. And now he's going to think Jews are boring.

He's met you. He's not going to think Jews are boring.

You laugh, but this is terrible. I'm moving them.

Grandma, please, no. Don't rearrange everything. Don't.

Why wouldn't I?

Because none of that matters anymore. His dad can think Jews are the worst people on earth and it wouldn't change anything. You know why?

Why?

Because I won. Charlie has no clean escape.

Ha!

THE MODEL

When you were seven years old, I took you to lunch on Worth Avenue in Palm Beach. In those days the boutiques had models parade by in the clothes and jewelry and talk to the ladies having lunch at the café tables along the sidewalks. Smart idea.

One of the women was walking past our table just *dripping* in costume jewelry—very practical for when you're traveling— and she stopped to smile at you. She thought you were cute, eating a plate of fries as big as your head. And she said, "Maybe your grandma would like to buy you one of these *lovely* brace- lets?" You looked her dead in the eye: "They're a little *clunky* for me," you said. Clunky. You must have heard me say it about something or other. Oh, how I laughed. The look on her face! They were terrible bracelets. You didn't have a bad eye.

I never treated you like a child. We didn't go to "children's" activities where I'd sit around while you painted this or that or ice-skated. I wasn't the grandmother who waited on a bench while you swung around on monkey bars. There's no equality in that. I never baked you a thing. What do I know about baking? I didn't read you books. You could read your own books! We'd read on the couch together from the time you were five. We'd go on outings to the museum and talk only about the art. We'd have quiche Lorraine in the cafeteria and you'd finish yours in three bites. Yes, we'd go to the beauty parlor, and while my color set you'd get your hair cut and blow-dried. But we also would talk about our friends and who was disloyal or a bore or going with the wrong boy. I'd take you to Neiman's to buy myself a suit for a party, and you'd give your opinion on the colors.

I raised you as my equal so I'd have a friend. Birds of a feather.

THE SLEEPOVER

Neither of us has ever been any good at falling asleep. We're wired the same. Always something to do. Something to read. To eat. To worry about. The two of us, lying awake at midnight, staring up at our ceilings, two minds whirring in the dark.

Do you remember Eleanor Porter? You adored her—she was a kind, polite child. You both read those historical fiction books about colonial dolls who came to life. Do you know whatever happened to her? You mustn't lose touch with your friends, honey. Look her up online.

Anyhow. When you were about eight years old you were over at Eleanor's house for a sleepover and you couldn't sleep.

You had tossed and turned in your sleeping bag on the floor, and you had worked yourself into a cold sweat. You got in your own head. What could you possibly be so stressed about at eight years old? Whether your dollhouse was up to code?

This had happened before. At that girl Rebecca's. At Claire's on her birthday. At Stephanie's just a few weeks before. Your mother had warned you it would happen again. She told you to leave after dinner. That she wouldn't pick you up later than ten. That you needed to "know yourself."

But you wouldn't accept defeat. Not on her terms. So dinner came and went and you felt fine. And you changed into your pajamas and you watched the movie with the other girls with your teeth grinding in your skull, and you felt the adrenaline rise in your chest and you readied yourself for lights out. You got into your sleeping bag and you were immediately in hell. The clock on the wall was ticking too loudly. The carpet beneath you had a staple in it you could feel through all your layers. The tag in your pajama pants was stabbing at you. You were doomed.

And there was no way you could call your mother. You refused to hand her this victory, no matter how desperately you needed to get into your own bed. But there was another way. Grandma.

It was eleven p.m. and you wriggled out of your sleeping bag and tiptoed down into the kitchen, picked up the phone, and dialed my number in Ardsley. It was one of the three numbers you knew by heart.

I was at the front door in my cream-colored Acura in thirty minutes. I insisted you tell the girl's parents—I didn't want everyone waking up and calling the police. You had to walk into their bedroom with your tail between your legs and tell them you were leaving. They didn't mind the late hour, they were sympathetic; Eleanor's mother was a kind woman.

You gathered up your things, handed me the sleeping bag, and I piled you into the backseat and drove you straight to your parents' house. It was only fifteen minutes away, but you were sound asleep by the time we pulled into your driveway.

I sat with the news on the radio and let you sleep like that for half an hour before I scooped you up and carried you inside like a rag doll.

You were eight, not some toddler. My back hurt for a week.

Your mother was in the living room wide-awake, of course. She'd been expecting your call.

PHONE CALL, 2015

GRANDMOTHER: I saw the most wonderful exhibit.
  GRANDDAUGHTER: *What was it?*

Klimts at the Neue Galerie. Bessie, you must go.
  Oh, I will. Next time I'm home.

You'll love them. It's extraordinary seeing them all together, room after room. As it should be.
  They have a Klimt at LACMA, I think.

Probably not a very good one.

THE MET

Do you remember what we always did when I took you to the Metropolitan Museum of Art?

I'd bring a yellow legal pad and pencils, and we'd sit in front of the paintings and you'd sketch.

"Bessarabia, what do you see?"

"Haystacks."

"I didn't realize I was accompanied by the chief art critic of *The New York Times*."

"What am I supposed to see?"

"You tell me."

And you'd get very close to the painting, your nose just a breath away from the varnish—the guards would bark at you and you'd jump back with an electric jolt and straighten your back, and we'd both wince and shrug at each other. And you'd collect yourself and clear your throat and stand there with your arms crossed, solemnly squinting at the painting, rocking from foot to foot like a grand appraiser. Thirty seconds. A minute. Five minutes. You'd occasionally stroke your chin with two fingers like you'd seen Bugs Bunny do in a cartoon. You might as well have wiped your monocle on a handkerchief.

Finally, when there was practically steam coming out of your ears, you'd have your fully prepared remarks: "I think he loved hay and he probably loved painting."

And I'd turn to the guard and say, "She charges fifty cents for a tour."

After the art was the main event: the cheese plate. We'd go to the grand old cafeteria where it used to be in the back of the museum in the columned atrium. We'd line up, pick out two plastic containers full of cheese, find a quiet table away from the tourists and talk, and eat our snack very methodically. First the brie, scooping it out from the rind with the water crackers, and then we'd press a sliced strawberry into the soft cheese and eat it just like that. We were very French, you and I.

We'd eat the cheddar, throw away the blue; then on the way out the main entrance you'd buy a postcard of your favorite painting. Always something with flowers.

. . .

METROPOLITAN MUSEUM OF ART,
PERMANENT COLLECTION, 1994

GRANDMOTHER: Bessie, I want you to go around these rooms and take this notepad and tell me how many paintings were done by a woman.

GRANDDAUGHTER: *And then we can look at the ballerinas?*

A building full of all the greatest masterpieces, and all you want is to see how an old man kept wandering into dance practice. I'd have had him arrested.

I like the ballerinas.

After this we can see as many damned ballerinas as you can stand.

[THIRTY MINUTES LATER]

OK! Eight women.

Eight!
Yep.

Did you write them down?

[STUMBLING THROUGH PRONUNCIATIONS]

*Simone Martini, Andrea del Sarto, Camille Corot, Annibale
Carracci, Andrea Mantegna, Jules Bastien-Lepage, Camille
Pissarro, and Jan Steen.*

Oh, honey. Give that here.

[EXTRACTS GLASSES FROM GIANT HANDBAG, LOOKS AT THE PAPER]

Did I miss any? I saw them all.

All of those are men.
They have girls' names.

They're just European names.
Did I miss the women?

There aren't any women.
It was a trick?

It was a lesson.
What's the lesson?

If you're born a man and halfway decent at something, everyone will tell you you're great. There's only one woman nearby. Right through here in the American wing.

[TAKES HAND AND WALKS ME INTO THE NEXT GALLERY]

Here she is. *Lady at the Tea Table.* Mary Cassatt.
  I like it.

Yes, you do. You know how you can tell a Mary Cassatt?
  How?

She was kind to her subjects. She left out their hips.

FAMILY WEDDING,
MID-CEREMONY, 2009

GRANDMOTHER: Bessie, your shoes!
   GRANDDAUGHTER: *What? What's wrong with my shoes?*

They're stilts!
   They're only three-inch heels!

Six inches.
   Would you like me to stand up and get a cab and go back to the hotel in the middle of the vows and change?

If I had my way, yes.
   You know what? I have a higher pair.

Ugh! I don't know how you walk in those things.
   They make the outfit.

A good outfit doesn't make you suffer.
   I'm not suffering. You're the only one upset by them. Shh. Can we talk about this later?

Oh, sure. We can talk about it when you're being carted into an ambulance with a broken ankle.
   I'm not going to break my ankle!

[WEDDING ATTENDEE TURNS AROUND AND SHUSHES]

   Sorry!

Don't apologize to him, Bess. He voted for Bush.

A LIGHT LUNCH

HENRY'S CAFÉ, 106TH AND BROADWAY, 2013

GRANDMOTHER: I'm not hungry.
  GRANDDAUGHTER: *Neither am I.*

I think I'll just have something light.
  Me, too. Probably a salad.

A salad is a wonderful idea. And maybe a cup of soup.
  They have a tomato soup.

Perfect.

  WAITER: What can I get you ladies?

Bessie?
  I'll have the tomato soup and then a chicken Caesar salad with the dressing on the side.

And I'll have the fried calamari and a hamburger medium rare.

  WAITER: French fries or onion rings?

A salad.

SHIRLEY TEMPLE

Bessie, you know I'd drop anything for you. Don't you remember what we did every Monday when you were in elementary school?

When you were in the third grade you started getting too nervous to go outside and play with the other children at recess. Every morning at around 11:30, right before lunch, you'd suddenly get a splitting headache and go lie down in the nurse's office. Eventually the nurse caught on to you and called your mother and refused to let you through the door. You could have been bleeding from the head and she would've turned you away.

You moved on to the librarian, Ms. Kingston. She loved having someone to talk to, I suppose. She'd recommend a book to you and you'd read it in three nights. She let you spend the lunch hour reshelving books. You learned the basics of the Dewey decimal system by age ten. You'd run out of books to organize and you'd move on to other projects. You made a giant banner spelling out READING IS FUN AND FUNDAMENTAL! You picked up on Ms. Kingston's mannerisms. You started wearing your hair piled high on your head like a Gibson girl and saying "Heavens to Betsy!" and you asked your mother for a fringed suede vest. Ms. Kingston started to feel badly for you. She called your mother and told her what was going on. But what was your mother to do? She was working! By that time she had a private psychiatry practice up and running and she had mental patients of her own to deal with. So you can imagine what happened. I got a call.

"Mom, Bess is a ball of neuroses. She refuses to go to lunch or recess."

"She just hasn't met the right people."

"She needs help."

"You're the psychiatrist."

"What am I supposed to do? She's crying every morning. She's refusing to go to school. On Sunday nights she can't sleep. She's getting these headaches."

"Headaches?" I'd heard that one before.

"Headaches."

Your mother and I both remembered how that went for her.

"Leave her to me. I have a brilliant idea."

The next day I showed up to the school at 11:30 a.m. and signed a form letter in the principal's office and then waited on a bench outside your classroom with *The New York Times,* just like I did when you were in nursery school. A bell rang at noon and the children filed out of the room and you were dead last, trudging behind the group, staring into the middle distance like a prisoner being sent to the gallows in pink corduroy pants.

I'll never forget the look on your face when I called out your name. "Grandma!" You rushed over and threw your arms around my waist, almost knocking me over.

"Bessie, we're going out to lunch."

We floated down the hallway, out the doors, and into my old Acura, and off we went. You never looked back. You didn't even ask where we were going. You buckled your seat belt and closed your eyes and inhaled your freedom, the smell of leather seats and my lipstick.

Ten minutes later we were sitting at café tables at a strip mall restaurant called Trio's. It was full of women with their baby strollers and middle-aged women drinking wine. There we were, two partners in crime.

The waiter came over. "What can I get for you ladies?"

"I'll have the Trio salad with no blue cheese and extra bacon."

You put down your menu. "And I'll have the same thing."

I raised an eyebrow.

"And what can I get you to drink?"

"I'll have a decaf iced coffee that's half milk, half coffee."

You paused. "Me, too."

"Bessie, you're going to hate it."

"No, I won't."

"Your mother will kill us both if she knows I'm letting you drink coffee."

"It's fine. It's decaf."

The waiter brought the salads. You watched me pour the dressing over the whole thing, then take my fork and spoon and mix it all together. So you poured your dressing over the whole thing and mixed it up the same way. Then I took a packet of Equal and dumped it in my iced coffee and mixed the drink with my straw. You did the same.

I folded my hands in my lap and watched you take a sip. You turned green.

"Bessie, am I ever wrong?"

You croaked out no before shoveling some bacon bits into your mouth to ease the agony.

I waved over the waiter. "She'll have a Shirley Temple."

"What's that?"

"Trust me."

The waiter brought over a stemmed glass with swirling pink grenadine spirals floating around the bubbles.

"Grandma?" you said, stabbing at the maraschino cherry with your little red straw.

"Yes, Bessarabia."

"Let's do this again tomorrow."

And we did.

And the day after that.

And the day after that.

Every day for the whole week. After that we went out to lunch and ate Trio salads every Monday for the entire year until you forgot you were afraid to go to school.

You're welcome.

On the day of my memorial service, you and your mother will go to the same shopping center, but Trio's will be gone. It will be a sushi place. You'll go in expecting it to look the same, to smell the same. Of course it won't. You'll sit down and your eyes will glaze over looking at the menu. Your mother will ask if you want to leave. You'll insist on staying. When the waitress takes your order, you'll ask, "Can you guys do a Shirley Temple?" You'll drink it through a straw in two big gulps.

THE PLAZA

Oh, how I loved taking you to Bloomingdale's when you were a little girl.

The point was we were going to a Broadway show or the ballet, but the main agenda was the shopping after. For us both. I'd pick you up at your parents' apartment—the tiny one on Eighty-fourth Street off Columbus. I put the down payment on it for your mother when she married your father; he was making nothing because he decided to go into research instead of opening a private practice.

So I'd pick you up and you'd be standing as soon as the buzzer rang. Of course I had the key to that one, too—your father couldn't stand that—but I'd knock on the door for the ritual of it. "Hello?" "Who is it?" "It's Grandma!" "Grandma who?" "Grandma Bobby!" "Just a minute!" Then you'd fidget with the lock and the handle, and there you'd be, in your Laura Ashley rosebud print dress.

It was your special dress. You wore it all the time. You wore it when I took you to the hospital when your brother was born. You wore it when you performed in your first play at your nursery school. All the children were supposed to wear black, and when I picked you up at the apartment, you looked so downcast in your sweatpants and T-shirt. "Bessie, this is your first play! Do you want to look like you're robbing a bank?" You turned around and stormed into your room. I thought you were furious. You closed the door. Two minutes later, you came out wearing your dress and a pair of white stockings and your white occasion shoes from Harry's on the Upper West Side. The whole outfit. You were panting, but you spun around and curtsied. I sat in the audience—your parents were working—and I had my wind-up camera and took a picture. Everyone needs the dress that makes her feel like she's able to do anything she wants.

On your fifth birthday, before we went to the ballet—it was *Swan Lake,* and I'll never forget it because you cried the whole

second act—I brought you down to the Plaza for tea. To the Palm Court. The soaring arched glass ceiling and palm trees growing in the middle of the room. You walked through those brass doors, your eyes big as saucers. "Grandma!" was all you said, and I said, "That's right."

You sat in a chair the size of a throne and I ordered a tea service for two. You looked at the sandwiches and you picked up the pink one and your face went green. I'd ordered raw salmon for a five-year-old who survived on nothing but noodles with butter! You looked at the plate on the table next to us. "Maybe we could have that also, please?"

I waved my hand for the waiter—they wore tuxedo vests, it was very elegant—and in under a minute, he brought a trio of sorbet surrounded by beautifully arranged fruit.

You ate each berry one by one. You picked up the kiwi and marveled. You'd never seen one! You took a little bite, then ate the whole thing in two mouthfuls. Your eyes teared up—you almost choked. You finished all the sorbet and closed your eyes.

I told you, "You know, Bessie, there's nothing I wouldn't do for you."

You were flushed from the cold and the excitement and I meant it. That's when you said it: "I love you, I love you, I love you."

And I said it back.

When I die you'll go to the Plaza. It will be on March 8, the third day of my shiva and what would have been my birthday. My ninety-first birthday. You'll have been prepared to cry all day. You'd cried at the funeral so hard you almost made yourself throw up. But on March 8, you'll wake up in your bed at your parents' apartment, take a shower, and put on a good silk blouse and a wool skirt and your opaque black tights and some ankle boots that are a little too masculine but at least they give you an inch of height.

You'll get dressed and very half-heartedly ask your mother if she needs you, and of course she'll say to go enjoy yourself. You won't tell your parents where you're going because you'll be vaguely embarrassed but also a little bit thrilled. You'll take a photograph of me out from one of the albums you took from the apartment after the funeral.

You'll put the old picture in your wallet and march down to West End Avenue and hail a cab. For once, you won't take the subway; you'll take a cab. Exactly as I'd insist. You'll walk into the Plaza with your head held high and you'll ask for "the room with all the palm trees," and somebody will escort you to the Palm Court. You'll ask the maître d', "Do you guys still

do the high tea?" "Of course, mademoiselle." Even though it's owned by some horrible conglomerate and half the rooms have been turned into condominiums, the Plaza's staff in the Palm Court will still be very well trained.

You'll take a seat and look around—a table of foreign tourists taking cell phone pictures, a few society mothers with their daughters—and you'll take the old photograph out of your bag very carefully and set it against the blue-and-white teacup on your table. You'll take a picture of the photograph. You'll order the tea for two with the Earl Grey and you won't even look at the price. You'll eat it all. Every bite. Even the salmon. God knows you don't need the scones, but you'll force them down. The waiter will come by to take the tray and the cup and he'll see you're crying. "Can I get you something, miss?" he'll ask.

You won't miss a beat and you'll tell him, "A Kir Royale." You'll drink about half and start to feel nauseated. All those scones.

You'll pay the bill, look at the photograph, and say, "Happy birthday, Grandma," and that will be that.

VOICE MAIL, MAY 2016

Yeah, hi—Bessie. It's Grandma. I'm reading *The New York Times* and I saw an article about cats. Are you sitting down? There's a toxin in their feces. It goes directly into your brain and it's apparently very dangerous. Anyway, they say it's bad for pregnancy. There are women in Brooklyn giving away their cats to shelters, which is very smart. I know you love the thing, but if you are handling Al's excrement and changing the litter box, you're risking all kinds of developmental problems and who knows what. Your mother says you and Charlie aren't *trying* to have a baby yet, but you never know how these things go and you don't want to screw yourself up in advance. Give away the cat. I'll mail you the article. You know what? I'll mail it to the cat.

IN THE CAR,
SOUTH OCEAN BOULEVARD, PALM BEACH, 2015

GRANDMOTHER: You know Miriam's granddaughter Becky has a night nurse for her baby, but Becky doesn't even work.
GRANDDAUGHTER: *Well, everyone needs to be rested.*

I didn't have a night nurse.
I guess that makes you a better person than Miriam's granddaughter!

I don't know how they get the money—Becky's husband is a *graphic designer.* Miriam and Al must pay for it. Which is fine.
Sure.

I just don't see why she can't be bothered to comfort her own child in the night. It's not like she has anywhere to be in the morning. Or let the kid cry it out! That's what I did.
That explains my mother.

You'll keep working after you have a child.
I don't know that. Maybe I'll fall in love with the baby and need to be with it all the time.

It has nothing to do with loving the baby. It's about living your life and remaining in the world. You don't want your child to be bored of you by age five.
No, I don't.

If you ever want a night nurse for your baby, I'll pay.

Grandma, by the time I have a baby, I'll figure out my own child care.

I'm getting you a night nurse.

YOUR BONES

I made you cry twice. It was the loudest and most horrible thing. Like a hyena. Both times, I cried, too.

The first was when you were a little girl. We were at a manor restaurant up the Hudson River for my birthday—my sixty-something or other. I loved my birthdays, all of them. It's a shame I died without properly celebrating my ninetieth. I was too ill. What a party that could have been. We'd have flown you all out. Probably the Breakers, like my seventieth. That was a party. Fifty years before that, they wouldn't have let a Jew set foot in the Breakers. Yet there we were, toasting the daughter of two shtetl immigrants underneath the crystal chandeliers and the ocean out the window.

So at the manor restaurant after my birthday lunch, we were all taking a family picture. You would always sit on my lap, and so I held on to you and the whole family gathered around. All of my children and their children. And I looked behind me and nobody was in the right place—your mother was in the back and I think your father was somewhere outside the frame. I was ordering everyone around and trying to get it arranged, and your mother started going at it with me and you slipped off my lap and walked away. You hated it when we fought. You headed toward the stone wall at the edge of the property, and what you didn't know—what I knew—was it was a sheer hundred-foot drop off a cliff down to the river. Everyone was settled and it occurred to me you weren't there, and I saw your white dress disappear across the lawn and got up and ran like a bat out of hell. My shoe got stuck in the grass, and I ran for you with one stocking foot soaking up the mud. *"Bessie! Stop!"* You turned around, looked right at me, and you just teetered on top of the stone wall, completely expressionless, the river running ten stories under you. You were paralyzed with fear just standing there. I launched at you, grabbed your forearm, and *yanked* you into me. Your shoulder went *pop!*

And you let out a howl. Real, round tears were streaming down your cheeks. You couldn't believe how much I hurt you. You glared at me so confused and then lay down on the grass in front of the stone wall in shock. Your father reset the bone right then and there—he had come running, too.

The second time you were much older. It was at the Home Port in Menemsha on the Vineyard. You made it out to the parking lot of the restaurant before you really let yourself go at it. You'd been recently married and were back from your honeymoon in France, where you insisted on staying in rented apartments instead of the great hotels, and we were having salads. It was the first course. You are normally so svelte, so petite, which is smart because you aren't very tall, but you had an appetite that summer and you were happy and you'd ballooned up. You'd gained probably five, six pounds. It doesn't sound like a lot, but on your frame . . . And you knew it. You wore a one-piece bathing suit for the first time since you were a little girl.

Anyhow, we were eating salads and yours was a wedge and

you dumped the dressing on top—all of it. I'd ordered it for you on the side for a reason. I noticed how your cheeks were too full and your arms weren't as lithe as they could be, and I told you, "Bessie—that's enough." You stopped moving entirely and you clenched your jaw.

Very slowly, you stood up. You wouldn't look at anyone. You walked straight past the Ballards, who couldn't imagine why anyone would be so dramatic—I had to tell them you had food poisoning—and you headed into the parking lot.

Your grandfather looked at me with such sadness. "Bob. Go to her."

I walked out of the restaurant, and there you were, slumped beside the car, crying into your hands. Snot and everything.

I felt very small across the parking lot from you, with you so far away. I walked to you and you glared at me. "Grandma," you said, "you can't say those kinds of things to me." I knew what you meant. I knew I was right, too. But I knew it didn't matter. You were furious—you wouldn't look at me. You looked straight at the ground. I'd never seen you like that. And I didn't know what to do.

You were an attractive girl, but a pound on the wrong side of the scale is noticeable because you're short. The weight always went to your hips, and the style was these skinny jeans, so there was no escaping it. You loved to eat. Always. I'd move the bread rolls at Thanksgiving. I'd push your plate away from you when you'd eaten a full portion. "Bessie, you've had enough!" It was a song I sang. I thought you were in on it.

Your mother blamed me for how much you took it to heart. She said it would harm you. That after a stomach flu when you lost four pounds in a week you told her, "Grandma would be proud," and she laughed but then she called me screaming.

So there you were, breathing deeply in and out, and you raised your head with red eyes, looking at me like I was a stranger. I had lost you. There's only one other person who's ever looked at me like that in my entire life. And I created *her,* too.

So I took both of your hands in mine and clutched them. I squeezed down hard, to remind you of me. I said what I always said: "Bessie, do you know how much I love you?"

You were about to say something, but all you could do was let out a very quiet gasp. And then we were both crying. We didn't hug; we held all four of our hands, all entwined, and yours covered in mucus.

We looked like nutcases. We were.

Then I said something I never said to your mother: "I'm so, so sorry." You said, "I know." You didn't forgive me. You didn't say, "It's okay." You just looked me right in the eye and said, "I know." I took you in my arms and smelled the top of your head and squeezed your ribs into mine.

And we went home and watched a Turner Classic Movie on my bed eating cinnamon rugelach right out of the container.

PHONE CALL, NOVEMBER 8, 2016

GRANDMOTHER: Bessie, I can't watch.

GRANDDAUGHTER: *Grandma, it's fine. They haven't counted Michigan.*

No.
It's not over.

My father.
I know.

My father would kill you if you weren't a Democrat.
Grandma, it's going to be okay.

My father would kill himself.
I know.

I'm so upset I could cry.
Don't cry. It'll be all right. There's no way he is going to be president.

You're wrong.
I know.

My father was a union organizer.
I know.

He used to stand on an overturned milk crate in Union Square.
I thought it was a soapbox.

Whatever it was. Doesn't matter.
Grandma, do you know what your zayde would say?

Now's not the time.
He'd say one foot in front of the other.

He'd show up at Mar-a-Lago with an elephant gun.

APARTMENT LIVING ROOM, PALM BEACH, 2015

GRANDMOTHER: It's fine, Bess. The mucus has to come up.
GRANDDAUGHTER: *You're barely able to catch your breath.*

It's good. It's fine. I'm getting it out. It's good.
Grandma, we should take it easy—let's eat at home. There's plenty of stuff in the apartment. I was up late—I'm tired, too.

Who said anything about being tired?
You're coughing too much. You're going through a pack of
tissues a day. It's not good—just don't push it. I need you.

I need you, too.
You have to rest.

Neither of us can sleep at night. Our brains keep going.
Maybe we should take something.

Then who would do the worrying?
My mother.

Your mother. Bessie, pat my back—
I got you. It's okay. Let it out.

Bessie?
Yes, Grandma.

Get my handbag. We're going out to lunch.

VERY ILL

I wasn't ill for very long before I died, but right before my
heart went out, I gave your mother jewelry. I showed her my
drawer in the bedroom in Palm Beach and I started putting all
of these pieces in her hands. I made her get a Ziploc bag when
she couldn't hold it all. It was mostly junk—all the diamonds

and fine pieces were in the vault. But I gave your mother my black pearl necklace, a pin from Russia, my clip-ons, the bangle I brought back from Italy, and my brass ring inlaid with colored stones the size of jelly beans. She didn't refuse like she usually did. She just said, "Thanks, Mom." A week later I lay down and that was that.

I knew and she knew. It's why I didn't call you. It's why I refused the phone when you called: you called your mom and asked her to give the phone to me and I wouldn't let her. You tried to video chat—you needed to see me. The last you saw of me was on the screen on your phone. The top half of my face, just my eyes. Your mother was holding it. I said, "Oh, Bess," and then, "Put it away, Robin."

The longest we ever went without speaking was the week and a half before I died.

I'd been sick on and off for years, but we didn't talk about it. We'd drive down South Ocean Boulevard and you'd take the wheel with one outstretched arm while I hacked into a tissue.

We never discussed our illnesses because we didn't want the other person to feel helpless. What was there to say? There was nothing either of us could do to fix it.

When you were diagnosed with ulcerative colitis in college, I couldn't stand it.

You lied to me almost immediately. You lied about the hospitalization—"I went in and saw a great doctor, they figured it out, and I'm on the right medication and I'm going to be fine." You told me it was curable. You lied about the pain and the blood and the gore. When Evan, that boyfriend you had, broke up with you two weeks later, all you told me was he wasn't coming to Seder. The rat bastard. I asked why not and you held the phone away from your head and I could hear you cry.

Your face became swollen from the steroids. You would lie awake at night sweating from the medicine and the fear, wondering if you'd die from it one day. Food would hurt you. Stress would hurt you. Your heartbreak hurt you. I should have killed him. Your grandfather almost did. "If I see him on the street, I'll break his skull." He really said that.

When you sank into a depression after the diagnosis, you didn't let me know. You became very thin. Your arms were like strings and your head bobbled on your neck. You dropped classes and you didn't tell me. I'd ask you how school was and you'd say, "Fine"—a lie. I'd ask when you were coming to Florida and you'd get very quiet. You couldn't see past the end of the day. You were in the dark.

You're like me. Easily upset. Easily stuck. Easy to cry. Easy to mope. Easy to lie through your teeth, to swallow the blood in your mouth and laugh.

We get to the point when our bodies won't let us hide inside them. And that's the only reason we die. I wouldn't let that happen to you. I told you, "Bessie. Drop out. It doesn't matter. You must do whatever makes you happy. Life's too long if you're miserable." You could beat your illness. You didn't have a choice.

When you came to Martha's Vineyard that summer, you brought your friend Katie, who is wonderful. She's a very good friend, Bessie. An "up" person. Always keep her close. God forbid you outlive Charlie.

So you landed in the dinky Cape Air plane on Martha's

Vineyard, and of course I was waiting in my spot right at the gate on the landing strip at the airport. And I was waving like a lunatic and you smiled a big, happy smile. And your face was like a chipmunk's—more than usual—and your eyes were sunken and you could barely pick up your backpack when the man took it out of the compartment on the wing. When they opened the gate, I ran onto the tarmac and pulled you into my arms and into my chest and your chin bobbed down on my shoulder, and I squeezed you until I felt your vertebrae pop. I held you so hard you could barely draw breath. *"I love you, I love you, I love you."* Then we held hands as we walked to the car and we didn't say a thing.

You know the story of my *zayde*. He was always dead broke and in trouble with a bookie, but he made it through the pogroms and the passage to America, and he kept living until everyone he knew was dead. And you know what he said—I'll say it again, I don't care if you've heard it a thousand times. I don't care if you can say it backward in French standing on your head. He told me, "Bobby, when the world is cracking behind your feet, you keep walking forward."

You march forward.

January, February, *March*.

We thought my lungs would do it, but it was my heart that went out in the end. My lungs were always the problem. Blame the smoking, though I never did. Blame the years bringing lunch to your grandfather's construction sites breathing in God knows what. Whatever it was, as I got older, they troubled me *constantly*. Your grandfather became very nervous when I'd cough in my sleep. He'd stay up at night watching me, tears in his eyes. I was intubated more times than you know.

I'd call your father sometimes very late at night—thank God your mother married a pulmonologist—and he'd listen to my breathing over the phone and he'd send me to the emergency room. I had operations. We never talked about it—you'd be so far away out in California. What was I going to do, ruin your day? So I'd let my phone go to voice mail until I could say the words: "I'm fine, Bessie. I'm fine." I'd leave enough of it out, but I wasn't lying.

In my last few years, everyone was sure of two things: I could go at any second, and I'd live forever. I'd let it slip to you when I was very tired—I'd taunt you with it: "You know, I'm not going to be around forever." You'd say your line: "Grandma, you're going to walk my children to preschool. You're going to torture them like you tortured me." When I was humoring you, I'd say, "Fine," and when I was feeling angry, I'd just say, "No." You can't say I was ever wrong.

I was always very active, as hard as it was. I'd walk every day. In Florida I'd put on my sneakers and get out of the building, and I'd walk down South Ocean Boulevard until the curve in the road, then I'd walk back. I'd walk with a friend and gossip, and when they all died, I'd walk with your grandfather. We didn't have to say much, but we walked. I walked at my pace—fast, head low, onward. Faster than him. He'd shout, "Bob! Slow down!" and I'd say, "Hank! Speed up!"

On the Vineyard we'd drive fifteen minutes from the house to Menemsha and park at the Galley and walk the dock. We'd go all the way to the end and back—sometimes twice if I was feeling spry and there wasn't too much wind. Before we got back to the car, I'd get a veggie burger from the take-out window and your grandfather would get the fried chicken wings.

Sometimes I'd get a soft-serve ice cream or French fries and a decaf iced coffee. Or we'd get calamari and onion rings for later. We earned it.

But by the end it was an accomplishment if I walked anywhere. I walked on the treadmill in the apartment in Florida very slowly—your mother watched me do that in the last days. "Mom! Slow down!" I'd get angry. It was very upsetting becoming so slow. To be stuck. For your body to beg you to stop. For nurses to come into the house and bathe me when I couldn't get out of bed. You can't imagine. You can't imagine the pain of becoming slow, of knowing it's as fast as you'll ever be again, of not being able to call you, of letting the phone ring until it stopped because I couldn't tell you I was all right. In my last week, you didn't hear from me. I didn't have anything to say.

You mustn't be so angry at yourself for not getting through to me in those last days. You'll never escape the knife blade of that guilt pressed to your throat. You must move forward. You're sorry and so am I. What are we supposed to do now? Talk about it? Ha. You can write all you want, but you're still at a desk in a world where I don't exist. I'm the way you think.

FACETIME CALL, FEBRUARY 27, 2017

THE LAST TIME I'LL SEE YOU

GRANDDAUGHTER: *Grandma, we got another cat! Look!*
His name is—

GRANDMOTHER: Ugh. You and the cats. Don't show me the
cats. We are *not* cat people.
Fine. How's Florida? How's the weather?

I'm so lonely. Everyone has died.
Don't cry. Don't cry. Everything's fine. Do you want me to
come down? I can be there tomorrow night.

Your mother is with me.
All right, so in that case you can cry.

Ha! She's worried.
That's her job.

That's my job.
That's my job. Are you sleeping at night?

No.
Are you eating?

Yes. I had a Reuben for lunch.
How was it?

It was fair.
Are you in any pain?

I'm just so upset. So tired.
Me, too. But there are wonderful things to look forward to.

Huh. Like what?
Charlie and I will have a baby someday.

Oh, Bessie. Oh. Oh.
And you'll be there to give it hell. To make it miserable.

Oh, how I want to.
Grandma?

My angel?
If you're not around when it's born, I'll kill you.

You have a deal.

part four

AFTER ME

WHAT HE'LL DO

I DON'T KNOW WHAT HE'LL DO, now that I've gone first.

Oh, how he needs me. Who will he talk to? Who will remind him to have lunch? The only thing he's ever made is a bowl of cereal. Even then, it's all milk. He'll have to hold your child and I won't be there. He'll cry. You'll cry. He'll have to walk by my makeup brushes in their silver jar on my bathroom counter. The brigade of orange medicine bottles with my name on them he'd picked up from the pharmacy just a few days before. He'll have to answer the phone. He'll have to watch movies alone. He'll have to button his cuffs. He'll have to see the sun go down and the sun come up. He'll be surrounded by the books I've read and he'll be envious of them, my old friends. He'll read a few pages of Didion and put it down. "What is this about?" He'll have to wonder about what was in my head. He'll have to live. He'll have no reason except the beating of his heart. The

lungs that fill and empty. The body that carries on at half-mast. He'll kiss the coffin like I'll feel it.

THE DAY I DIE

You'll be alone in the car when you get the call from your mother at around four p.m. on a Friday. Thank God you'll already be pulled over. It would've been two of us dead in a day.

You and Charlie will have been driving back from a night in Malibu—you had the day off from work. "You know what you do when you're feeling blue? Check into a hotel." "I can't afford to do that." "Use my card." You'll have checked into a cheap rental apartment off the Pacific Coast Highway instead. It made Charlie more comfortable, and by that point that's what matters to you.

Two things will happen that Friday morning at the beach in Malibu that will be very unusual in retrospect. Or maybe they won't. Every detail takes on a certain foreboding air before a disaster.

You'll take your paddleboard out beyond the pier and you'll see a dolphin in the distance behind a white buoy. For whatever reason, you'll decide that dolphins come in pairs, so if there's one there must be another and you want to find out. You'll paddle fast—too fast!—to the place where it crested out of the water. You shouldn't be out there alone. It's the open ocean! A wave could tip you over and you could hit your head and drown and that would be the end. Dead and floating with a strap around your ankle. Who needs a wave? You could lose your balance for no reason at all! You've never been a natural athlete.

So anyway, you'll go after this dolphin, and of course it will have long disappeared. And you'll be out of breath, and at the buoy you'll sit down on the board and tuck the paddle under your leg, and a seagull will land right on the buoy in front of you. You'll be startled. "Hello!" It will look right at you. And you'll look right at it. You two will hold your glare, but you'll get spooked and you'll get up and paddle away. You'll look over your shoulder after a minute or two and it will have disappeared.

Right around then, back on the shore, Charlie will lose his phone. He'll be jogging on the sand and it'll fly out of his pocket directly into the ocean. *Bop!* Destroyed in a chaotic instant. He'll be very embarrassed—it's not the kind of thing that happens to Charlie. It's a matter of pride how he keeps his *things*. You'll get back to shore and he'll explain the situation, and you'll dry off and load into the car to go to the store on the way home and try to haggle for a new one. You'll find street parking outside the Verizon store at Wilshire Boulevard and Twenty-sixth Street in Santa Monica. You'll sit there with your feet up on the dashboard while Charlie goes in to make his case for a free upgrade. "Don't talk to strangers," he'll deadpan. You'll be generous and laugh.

So you'll be alone in the passenger seat, staring at your phone. And your mother will call. And her voice will be quiet and light. She'll speak to you like a child.

"Bess—Bess?"

Something will be strange.

"Grandma Bobby had a heart attack in the middle of the night and she passed away."

"Passed away." Not "she died."

"She passed away." A euphemism. The implication of a destination.

She passed away in the middle of the night.

And "Grandma Bobby" was very odd. Your mother had only ever said "Grandma." Never once "Grandma Bobby." So there it is: "Grandma Bobby had a heart attack in the middle of the night and she passed away."

You'll have two responses.

The first is a howl. It will be very low—a siren.

"Stop," your mother will say. "You'll make yourself sick."

She'll really say to stop. Stop crying. You'll become furious immediately. You'll say something very theatrical, using her shrink-speak against her.

"Mom, how dare you police my grief?" My granddaughter, Scarlett O'Hara.

Then you'll cry with your mouth open into the phone, gasping and trying to breathe. Eyes bulging out like a trapped bear. If someone had looked in the window, they'd have thought your leg was caught in the door.

Your mother will say what she always says to you when she's trying to calm you down: "You're on speakerphone with Dad."

"Where was Grandma?"

"She was at home."

"She died at home?"

"She died in the hospital. She had the heart attack at home and they took her to the hospital."

"Who took her to the hospital?"

"Grandpa and the nurse."

"She was with some *nurse*?"

"And Grandpa."

"Was Grandpa there when she died?"

"I don't know. He was in the hospital. But she was in the ER, so—"

"She was scared."

"She was so out of it—she'd had ministroke after ministroke and had been degrading for weeks and this was her time."

First "passed away" and now "her time." Don't blame your mother. There isn't any way to talk about death that isn't a little bit automatic.

"Where is she now? Is Grandpa with her?"

You'll mean the body. My body.

"Grandpa was with her all night. Your uncle said it was very sweet. He was holding her hand."

Of course he was. Your grandfather held me with his whole

body until I was cold. Your mother wouldn't tell you for months, but he fought the doctors. He spent the entire night holding my body and shaking. The nurses had to wheel us both into a private corner of the ER. "Sir, I'm so sorry for your loss, but legally we have to move forward and we need the bed." "Go to hell. I need the bed."

"What time was it? What time did she die?"

"Two in the morning. Maybe three."

"Last night? Why didn't you tell me? I was paddleboarding all day like a fucking idiot."

There was a long pause. "I wanted you to have a few hours."

Then your mother started to cry. This is when you changed.

"Oh, Mom. I'm so sorry, Mom. I'm so sorry. Mom. Mama, I'm so sorry. She's your mom."

It was your mother's turn to gasp and sob.

Then you both cried and cried together, as your father said some more things about cognitive impairment after a stroke and the painlessness of sudden cardiac arrest.

Then Charlie got in the car with his bag from the Verizon store.

You looked at him with the phone in your lap and said, "My grandma," and he threw himself around you like you were on fire.

ONE WEEK DEAD

It's very odd what you'll take from my apartment the week I die. It will be during the shiva—the second day—and you'll be on a mission for nothing in particular. Whatever seems to call out to you. A thief on a blind scavenger hunt, tomb raiding for tchotchkes. You'll take a paper grocery bag from under the sink and walk room to room, while your mother sits on the sofa in the living room staring at her phone.

Three white cotton handkerchiefs with a floral needlepoint embroidered in the corners.

A tiny porcelain Limoges egg with a brass hinge in the middle.

An orange-and-blue silk Pierre Cardin scarf stained with brown makeup along an edge.

A size 8 pin-striped thick cotton button-down Brooks Brothers shirt.

A retractable makeup brush inlaid with pink and orange enamel squares.

A small gold Estée Lauder makeup compact full of pressed powder and the applicator puff.

A bright coral Yves Saint Laurent lipstick.

A copy of my wedding invitation from a scrapbook.

A menu from my wedding dinner.

A copy of my first learner's permit.

A picture of me at your age laughing on a boat next to an American flag.

A blue Bic pen from my bedside table missing the cap.

Another lipstick. Chanel. Rouge Coco.

.   .   .

It'll be difficult to imagine your mother as a particularly affectionate grandmother. She could barely hold you when you were a baby. You were always falling out of her arms, wriggling free, one leg sticking out to the ground, her hand hoisting you by the crotch. She didn't indulge you. She waited until you were done talking and then went into another room, relieved and amused, wondering if you were falling behind in math.

Here's what I predict:

She'll drop everything for your child. She and your father will move to L.A. They'll both be retired and she's been planning it for years. She'll rent an apartment and she'll wait for your calls. "Mom?" She'll take the child to school—she'll have her own car seat for the baby that's better than yours, and a backup just in case—driving 5 miles an hour, talking sweetly the whole way in a voice that will seem alien to you. She'll wait patiently outside the child's classroom, reading *The New York Times, The Wall Street Journal, The Washington Post* on her iPad. She'll learn a new smile, the smile for your baby. She'll take the baby on long walks and talk to them right into their eyes. She'll notice the child likes peas and your freezer will be full of peas. There will be endless shopping bags full of bibs and swaddles, plastic stroller attachments in boxes you'll never open. You wait.

If you have a daughter, your daughter will fight with you the way you fought with your mother and the way your mother fought with me. She'll scream bloody murder when you don't take her side. She'll need your approval and you'll be impossible to please. She'll tell you she hates you. She'll mean it with all her heart. Her face will turn red and her mouth will go tight. She'll storm off and slam her door and you'll hear her cry on the other side. The whole thing. You won't follow her; you'll close your own door and cry. Charlie will go to you the way your father went to your mother and your grandfather went to me, and she'll resent you for it, not him, never him, the saint, the captive. She'll call you "Bess" once and you'll scream, "I'm your mother!" "No, you're not." Yes, you are. That's when you'll know. Yes, you are.

She'll prefer your mother to you by the time she's ten. Daughters can't wait to get away from their mothers. They can't wait to fall into their grandmother's arms.

Don't say I never told you so.

ONE YEAR AND THREE MONTHS DEAD

THE GRAVE

You'll be writing this the morning you visit my grave for the first time since I died.

It's a good lead-up to the sight of my grave plot. The book distances you from my death. It summons me right into your head. "What were her stories? What would she say?" It's turned me into a riddle, a series of boxes to unlock, pages to riffle through in your mental filing cabinet. Bess, I'm not a riddle—I'm a corpse. In a horrifying flash you'll wonder what I look like and you'll banish the thought immediately, burying it until a nightmare digs it up.

You'll get on the Cape Air flight with Charlie and fly to the Vineyard and take a taxi to the cemetery.

You'll remember the coffin from the funeral with its Jewish star. How your grandfather kissed it after he spoke. How very sad the funeral was for an old lady's death. Nobody could

have predicted how the fact of my age became the enormity of the loss—the weight of my absence. Ninety years and three-hundred-something days. That's a long time to be stomping around, collecting all the people who'd gathered around in black clothes to stare down at my headstone.

You've been easing in and out of your grief for a year, and it's not stopping you in your tracks anymore. You don't pause in front of the mirror and wonder if I'm looking through your eyes. You don't let the air catch in your chest when you see an old lady about my height, a shopping bag in her hand. When you smell a lipstick or wonder if you should have brought a warm layer to the movie. You talk about me constantly to Charlie, who's very patient and smiles. "My grandma would love this hotel." "My grandma would hate these boots." "My grandma would never forgive me if I stayed home." "One foot in front of the other."

You've reached for me privately when you've been scared.

"Grandma, please make the colitis flare go away tomorrow."
"Please don't let the plane go down." "Please help me merge
onto the freeway." I have no control over any of that. What am
I—a magical ghost? If the plane goes down, don't blame me.
The last thing I need.

The grave plot is perfect. High enough on the hill with
nobody behind it, bigger than the ones around it, except for
the Cohens', which is gargantuan. You'd think they're obese.
I don't know why they planted beach roses next to it. They'll
rot! Somebody has to water them. It's unnecessary. What can
you do?

I'm to the right and your grandfather will be to the left,
which is the opposite of how we slept, so that's unfortunate.
Nobody asked. He'll say, "I wanted them to carve my name in
it, too," and he'll mean it in every sense. The year hasn't done
a thing for him.

You'll see my name in the stone—BARBARA OTIS BELL.
And then the inscription that reduces us to our familial roles,
a woman's chronology: BELOVED WIFE, MOTHER, GRAND-
MOTHER, AND GREAT-GRANDMOTHER. Beloved wife. That's
true. Beloved mother. Depends who you ask.

1926 TO 2017. They're the mortal years. The ones from
when I cried out on my mother's dining room table to when I
lurched under the defibrillator in the hospital as your grandfather barked orders against my express wishes. The years I
could hold my mother and your mother and you.

You'll look at the ground and it will become very clear that
I'm not there.

What have I always told you, Bessie? What have I always
said? You're my angel. I am you. I'm the bones in your body

and the blood that fills you up and the meat around your legs. I'm the softness of your cheeks and the way they freckle in the summer, and I'm the streaks of rust in your hair, and I'm the nose under your nose and the eyes that narrow with fire and roll backward in delight at all the same things. I'm your style. I'm your laugh. I'm the rage in your heart that I'm not here. You're the body I left behind.

I made sure of that. From the moment I met you, I never stopped telling you my stories. Because nobody will write them but you.

ONE YEAR AND SIX MONTHS DEAD

GRANDDAUGHTER: *I miss you.*

GRANDMOTHER: I miss you, too, Bessie.
I wish I could hear you.

Listen to the voice mails.
I'd rather not.

There's gray in your hair.
Not really.

Yes, there is. All throughout. You can't see it in the back.
I'll dye it.

No, you won't.
I will if it's that noticeable.

I went gray very young, and the key is to keep the tone light.
Blend it in. Your mother kept hers dark so her roots were
always showing.
   Okay.

You're not going to dye it, are you?
   Probably not. Charlie doesn't mind it.

Of course he minds it.
   Oh, you can read people's thoughts from beyond the grave?

Don't be cute. No man wants to see his wife age.
   He's not like that.

They're all like that.
   Grandma?

Yes, dear.
How did everything change with you and my mom?

I've told you a thousand times.
Tell me again.

I showed up at the hospital a few hours after you were born. Your mother was asleep in the hospital bed, and your father was sitting beside her, and you were in the bassinet next to the bed. And I was very quiet because I knew she'd kick me out if I disturbed anyone. So I tiptoed over to see you. And, oh, Bess. You were the most beautiful child. They called you "the beautiful one" in the nursery—I swear on your life. Big fat cheeks and a little cupid's-bow mouth. We squawked at each other, and I held you and we locked eyes and I called you my angel.

Then your mother woke up. And she sent your father out into the hall. I was ready for her to give me hell. She and I had a rough go of it while she was pregnant with you. As soon as I had one opinion about your nursery, I was the villain of the century. And so we'd hardly been talking, but of course I showed up that morning. I'm not a terrible mother.

And so it was just the three of us, and there I was holding you and she said, "Come over." And so I did. And I handed you to her. And she laid you on her chest and you nuzzled right into it. And she looked at me and she had tears in her eyes and she said, "Mom?" And I said, "Robbie?" And she said, "What do I do now?" So I told her, "All you have to do is keep her alive." And then she patted the side of her bed, and I sat down on it right next to the two of you and she rested her head on my shoulder. She had never done that before. And that was that.

ONE YEAR AND SEVEN MONTHS DEAD

THE GODSEND

It'll take a year and two months for your grandfather to find someone else. It'll be Miri. My friend. My good friend. Some friend. What am I supposed to do, haunt her? That's your job.

Oh, please. I'm only joking. Calm down.

Everyone will be nervous about how to tell you. Your mother will call.

"I got us a great hotel room in Martha's Vineyard for when we visit."

"Why wouldn't we stay at the house?" A pause. You'll know why.

"Grandpa's friend is staying there."

"Oh? Who?" You'll be so casual you could blow away in the wind.

"Miri Pollack."

"Of Al and Miri?"

"Al died."

"That's right. She has to come that weekend?" A little attitude. Fine.

"She's staying the summer. She's leaving when Grandpa leaves."

"I think that's nice. That's very good."

"Yes, it's very good." She'll say it through her teeth, smiling at the wall.

"It's great. Whatever keeps him happy."

"He seems very happy."

"You know what—thank God."

"Right. Thank God."

"It's great. It's better than a nurse. It's someone to take care of him."

"So he's not lonely."

"It's so important."

"So important."

Another pause. You'll both lie down on your respective couches.

"Does she have her own money?" Good girl.

"I don't know. I think she's comfortable."

"She's not taking advantage of him."

"Lawyers made sure she can't touch his money."

"Okay." A pause. "Was Miri at Grandma's funeral?"

"I can't remember."

And then your mother will say the line. The line I'm sick of hearing.

"It's what Grandma would have wanted."

You'll let it hang in the air. And you'll hear me right behind you. I'll whoosh through your head in a gust of rage. You'll save it for later. "What Grandma would have wanted."

It's come up a few times since I died—about the jewelry, about the grave plot, about the ice cream sodas at the funeral.

What did I always tell you? I don't want another woman living in my house and wearing my jewelry. Your mother made sure she wouldn't be able to get her hands on any of it. But the house—what's he supposed to do? Put her up in a hotel?

Miriam had been in the house before. Many, many times. She and Al and your grandfather and me, eating swordfish and drinking sparkling wine on the porch.

You'll unpack at the hotel, and you and your mother will

drive to the house and pick up sandwiches for everyone on the way.

You'll steel yourself for the sight of her on my couch, at my table, on my chair, wherever. You'll tell yourself it's platonic. You'll keep using the word "companionship." But you know your grandfather. How he is. How he'd look at the old ladies at the bar in the front room of Ta-boo on Worth Avenue. "A pickup bar," and he'd wink.

You'll be very polite with her. You'll make a big show of it. You'll put her at ease.

"Miriam, it's *wonderful* to see you." "Wonderful": one of my words.

"Miriam, we brought you a turkey sandwich. Do you like turkey?"

"Miriam, do you have any great-grandchildren?" You'll tune out during her story and nod along at the pauses.

You'll do what I'd do. What my mother would have done. You'll hug her.

You'll feel her bones under her polo shirt. She won't hold you back, the way I pressed us together with a furious grasp. And you'll sit at the table with your mother and your grandfather and her. You'll notice her tenderness toward him. How she hands him a napkin when mustard drips on his chest. She won't mop it; she'll let him do it.

She'll clear her plate and his, making herself useful. "Does anyone need anything else?"

Your grandfather will announce to the air: "Miriam and I usually go for a walk after lunch."

Your mother and you will exchange a glance. It was our walk, the walk on the dock.

"It's windy," Miriam will say. "I'll bring us some sweaters."

You'll remember what your mother had said on the way to the house: "She's a godsend." What a word.

At the restaurant later that night, she'll thank the waitress after your grandfather barks his order. She'll order exactly the same thing as him and pile her French fries onto his plate. She'll laugh when he tells his stories about the chair that wobbled and the Mafia man taking his car. She'll wait as he tries to retrieve a name—as he closes his eyes and shakes out the memory. "It was Roy Bloch!" She'll exhale and smile. He'll offer her a bite of ice cream, which she'll accept, and he'll smile as she eats it.

As you and your mother get on the boat to leave, you'll wave back at both of them, smiling as they see you off. You'll realize it's the first time in over a year you've been with your grandfather where he hasn't cried. You'll watch the two of them turn around, hand in hand, and go back to the car to drive home. To watch the Yankee game, to read the paper, to go to bed and to wake up and to eat and to walk and to remember to bring each other a sweater.

And as the boat pulls away you'll say it to your mother: "It's what she would have wanted."

·   ·   ·

You know what I would have wanted? If you're asking me, I have a few ideas:

A plate of calamari and a decaf iced coffee.

A walk arm in arm with your grandfather on the dock in

Menemsha on a warm day and I don't have to stop and catch my breath.

The end of a decent book at two in the morning and a walk into the kitchen for a piece of chocolate babka.

A sale at Neiman's and a new lipstick—a neutral for fall. A mauve.

An ice cream soda.

A movie.

A new hat.

A new ending.

To go back to the last day.

To tell the nurse good night. To lie down in the hospital bed in the living room. To have the heart attack. To hear the emergency workers scramble the stretcher through the apartment, scuffing the marble with black treads. To be loaded on, breathing and not breathing. To ride in the ambulance with your grandfather strapped to a chair. To zoom through the ER, hear the shouting, your grandfather in hysterics; to feel the shock on my chest; to see my mother and your mother and you; and to look into your grandfather's eyes. To gasp. To hear the beep. *Beep. Beep.* Steady. To exhale. To laugh. To hear your grandfather wail, "Oh, Bob. Oh, Bob. I thought that was it."

For that not to be it.

To wake up the next morning and choke on the smell of all the flowers. To see you all there—whoever could make it. To see you cry. To hold your hand. My angel, my angel. To tell you to calm down. To not get hysterical. To see you laugh. "If you died, I'd kill you." To hear the doctor so proud of himself. "You gave us quite the scare, Mrs. Bell."

To go home in a taxi the next day. To send home the nurse. To send you back to work—to send you back to Charlie. To kiss you and kiss you and thank you. To make a roast beef sandwich and sit down at the kitchen table and split it with your grandfather. To call you and tell you about it. "What did I tell you?" "You'll be fine." "Would I ever lie to you?" "No, Grandma."

To put on a suit and my earrings and a brooch and go out to eat, to see the orchestra. To fly to the Vineyard. To check on the rosebushes outside the bedroom. To walk on the dock and to see Miri and Alice and Bob—that's all who's left. To hear an author's lecture at the community center. To mark the date on my calendar when you'd arrive. To wait at the gate at the airport and wave like a maniac as you and Charlie walk down the tarmac. To take you to lunch at the Galley and tell you to take the bread off your veggie burger. To see you shoot Charlie a look and shoot me a look and eat the bread anyway. To take you to the flea market and yell at you about a peasant top— you'll look like a tent. To sit on the couch with you and read our books. To tell you about my brother and how he insisted I learn how to read. To tell you about your mother and how she and your uncle tried to start a restaurant on the island. How they cut up skate with cookie cutters and sold them as scallops. To see your eyes crinkle when you laugh. To see a little gray in your hair in the light.

To send you off. To hug you until our bones crunch together. To wave at the gate in the parking lot as your plane takes off.

To get the call from you on February 13, 2019, when you find out you're pregnant with a healthy boy. A boy! To tell you that you caught a lucky break. To wait every day for any news. To show all my friends the pictures of the ultrasound. "He has his mother's old nose." To call about strollers and how the cheaper ones break and the child could fall and split his head wide open on the pavement. To hear you sigh. To insist it's true. To hear you laugh. To talk about schools and Los Angeles and how the air is terrible. To tell you to give away the cat. To tell you to find a nanny you trust, to name him something normal, to practice breathing. To tell you my mother gave birth on the dining room table. To laugh when you tell me there's no dining room table at Cedars-Sinai. To wait for the call. To fly out. To sit there in the waiting room with your mother. To hold the baby. To kiss you on your damp forehead and tell you how wonderful your life is about to become. To watch him grow. To say "I told you so" when you're back in New York in six months. To watch him walk and talk, and on his birthday—I'd be ninety-five—to walk with the two of you to school. "This is my grandma," you'd say. "She brought me to my first day and she's bringing my son."

To call you. To hear the phone ring and it's you. To tell you I love you. To tell you goodbye. To hear you say it back. "I have to die." "I know." "Is it okay, Bessie?" "Of course."

Oh, Bessie. My sweet Bessie. That's your fantasy. That's what you would have wanted. That's you at the center of it. It's only part of it.

You don't have any clue what I would have wanted.

You don't know how terrible it was at the end. How it hurt. How the strokes were happening and there was one doctor after another. How the indignity of old age defined me to everyone else but you. To myself. The face in the mirror with hollow eyes, so tired from the insomnia, then the naps, then the blood vessels bursting from the coughing. The erasure of all my beauty, like someone took a sponge to it. "Who is this old woman?" I didn't know. I could hardly hold my lipstick.

What would I have done with another minute of it, Bessie? Another day? Another two days? More doctors treating more conditions. More nurses with their impatient questions, their bored looks, thinking about their lunch break. More collapse, more parts of myself to go: my eyes, my hearing, my bowels, my mind. More panic in your grandfather's chest as he watched me struggle for breath at all hours of the night. More of the desperate thwarting of the inevitable decline. More alienation from a world I loved so fiercely, where I couldn't participate at all.

More of the same meals at the same places. More books on my chest as I fell asleep, none of them as good as they used to be, harder to read with their fine print. More names in my phone book crossed out, erased. Sitting there with the receiver in my hand, hearing the dial tone, no one to call. More voice mails to leave. More papers to read. More worrying about your mother and you. More minutes, more hours, more days that grew more labored. A stay of execution. A stopped clock.

What I would have wanted?

I thought about it the week your mother visited, when I handed her my jewelry to give to you. When I knew I wouldn't wear it anymore. That was the abdication.

You know what I would have wanted? I got it at the very end.

I wanted to fall into a very deep sleep.

She's crashing.

To wake up in silk pajamas in a big bed at a grand Parisian hotel. To light up a cigarette and breathe it all the way in.

Bobby! Bob! Oh god, oh god.

To sit on the bow of a sailboat, your grandfather at the tiller, cawing back at the gulls.

Oh god. Oh my god.

To twirl in a yellow skirt on a dance floor at a sorority mixer. To fall into your grandfather's arms. "Watch your step, Carmen Miranda!"

To step out of our gold Jaguar as the valet takes my hand. To walk through the doors of the country club for the first time, breathing in the clean marble and the smell of the lilies bursting from the flower arrangement on the lobby table. "Right this way, Mrs. Bell."

Do it.

To open my bathroom door to find your mother flushing my cigarettes, tears in her eyes: "Mom . . ." To watch you smile at me in the dressing room mirror, dressed in blue: "I love it, Grandma."

To feel Georgie walk across the room in the attic in Brooklyn. To hear him crouch over me and whisper, "My pet." To feel him kiss my little forehead and to feel my fever break, a cool mist lifting from my skin into my nightgown.

Charging!

To shout *"L'Chaim!"* at the chuppah as your mother kissed her husband, and her husband, and as you kissed yours. To watch your grandfather lifting the veil over my head, whispering, "How lucky am I."

Clear!

To be a little girl, floating on a tire attached to the dock, so sure I'd never drift away.

Clear!

To see my mother's face, flushed and wet, her hair matted to her forehead, looking at me with a love I'd never seen.

To die with every memory alive.

Every memory in you.

Every story to tell.

My story.

And my mother's story.

And your mother's story.

And your story. And your child's.

And for you to live so much and then for you to die.

And to leave the stories behind, to scatter them in the wind. The myths and the legends and the truth and the heart.

And they'll live on and so will I.

EPILOGUE

GRANDDAUGHTER: *Grandma, tell me about your mother.*

GRANDMOTHER: You tell me.
   I can't.

You're the one writing this.
   You are.

Of course I'm not. I'm in a box in the ground. You're putting words in my mouth. In a dead woman's mouth.
   Are you angry?

It's fine. Do you have a publisher?
   I don't know. Some people emailed me about it after the New Yorker *article.*

The article that was only on the internet.
That's right.

Not in the magazine.
Nope.

Did you get a lawyer?
I got a lawyer.

A good lawyer.
I think so. I certainly hope so!

That's how they get you in publishing. You must have a good lawyer look over the contract.
Grandma. Please. It's fine.

Bessie, do you know how much I love you?
Loved me.

Is it gone?
You're gone.

So what's the point?
I don't know.

Well. Do you know what my *zayde* used to tell me?
Yes.

When the earth is cracking behind your feet and it feels like the whole world is going to swallow you up, you put one foot in front of the other and you keep going. You go forward. And do you know what happens if you don't?

No.

Ha! Neither do I, angel. Neither do I.

AUTHOR'S NOTE

Although this book is nonfiction, oral history is by nature an imprecise exercise. *Nobody Will Tell You This But Me* is not an objective account of my grandmother's story, but rather a representation of a life, an echo, an impression, shaped and blurred through two generations and many retellings. Some names and identifying details have been changed. The major events described in this book happened and were verified through interviews with my mother and grandfather. I have brought as many tools as I could to this story, including the documentation, voice-mail recordings, and memorabilia on these pages. But this is neither my grandmother's memoir nor her definitive biography. She had three children and seven grandchildren, whom she loved fiercely. This story accounts for only two of those people. It's a matrilineal love story, drawn from her life, and dedicated to her memory.

ACKNOWLEDGMENTS

This book would not have been possible without my mother. Though she insists she'll never read it, it should be known by those who do that the book would not be here without her support and generosity. I am grateful for the hours she spent recounting stories from her childhood and young adulthood while I wrote. Thank you, Mom, for your unwavering (I think?) belief in me.

My dad was the book's first reader. Though he is a minor character in this text, it's his opinion that matters the most to me about most things. Thank you, Dad, for your help with this, and all things. You are a most excellent faja.

I also thank my grandfather Hank Bell for his support of this project on every level, and in particular for allowing me to record interviews with him about his career. Nobody's life was more profoundly shattered by Bobby's passing than his. My hope is this book is a comfort to him in a small way after the heartache he has endured every moment of every day since March 2017.

Thank you to Jeannie Otis, for her recollections of George, Leo, Rose, and Sam.

The book was brought into being by Robin Desser at Knopf. Robin's insight, judicious cuts and notes, faith, and encouragement transformed the book from its first draft into its current incarnation. I thank Robin for being my champion throughout this process. This book simply would not exist without her. Thank you, Robin.

Thank you to Erin Malone at WME for encouraging me to submit the proposal, and believing there was a book in my grandmother's stories and voice. It is due to her that the book ever saw the light of day.

Thanks to the brilliant Annie Bishai at Knopf for her excellent editorial notes and feedback on the manuscript, and for working so assiduously on behalf of the book. Annie, the book is better for your involvement in it.

Thank you to Katy Nishimoto for your sharp and formative notes on the very first draft.

Thank you to Victoire Bourgois, Lucas Wittmann, Kelly Dreher, Bridger Winegar, Jeff Loveness, Whitney Graham, and Katie Okamoto for your comments on early drafts of the book.

Thank you to Jimmy Kimmel for showing me how to work hard and do everything at once.

Thank you to Zoe Komarin for your reassurance through this process, with your wisdom, generosity, and pita. I love you.

Thank you, Will Kalb. There's nothing I wouldn't do for you, including leave you out of this book entirely.

Thank you to my son for allowing me to finish this book while pregnant with you. A lesser baby would have made that impossible.

Thank you to Charlie for getting me here. The boy and I are so glad to be loved and tolerated by you. You are the reason for all of it. How lucky am I.

LIST OF ILLUSTRATIONS